Infinite Power
for
Richer Living

Joseph Murphy, D.D., D.R.S., Ph.D., LL.D.
Fellow of the Andhra Research University, India

Parker Publishing Company, Inc.   West Nyack, N.Y.

DEDICATED TO ALL SINCERE SEEKERS
OF RICHER LIVING

Other Books by the Same Author

The Amazing Laws of Cosmic Mind Power
The Cosmic Power Within You
Miracle of Mind Dynamics
Power of Your Subconscious Mind
Your Infinite Power to Be Rich

What This Book Can Do for You

There is an Infinite Power within *you* that can lift you up, heal you, inspire you, guide you, direct you, and set you on the high-road to happiness, freedom, peace of mind, and the joy of fulfilled and triumphant living.

Based on my consultations and lectures in many countries of the world, I have noticed one great difference between people in all walks of life. Some of them are happy, joyous, successful, and prosperous; while others are unhappy and frustrated, and can't make ends meet.

Vast numbers of people in all walks of life go forward day by day, achieving and accomplishing great things. They are vital, strong, and healthy, and are contributing countless blessings to humanity. They seem to be imbued or possessed with some *primal force* that constantly works for their benefit.

Countless others, however, are leading mediocre, dull lives, full of burdens, in quiet desperation. They seem to have an inability to meet triumphantly and victoriously the challenges of life to win its satisfying rewards.

WHY YOU NEED THIS BOOK

This book teaches you how to meet and overcome the frustrations and problems of life. Each chapter reveals to you that every problem is always Divinely outmatched, and shows you how to rise strongly and victoriously above the problem into the dawn of a new day and a satisfying new life.

This book explains how to contact the Infinite Power within you and *supplies you with specific techniques for putting It into operation.*

It is for the express purpose of teaching the reader how to align and communicate with this Infinite Power and how to use It in his daily life that I wrote this book. I have endeavored on every page to explain the great basic, fundamental, and unlimited powers of your mind in the simplest and most direct language possible.

I urge you to study this book sincerely, and to apply the many effective techniques suggested and programmed in it. As you do this I am convinced that your mental contact and communication with this Infinite Power within you will cause you to rise confidently above confusion, misery, melancholy, and failure.

This Infinite Power will unerringly guide you to your true place, solve your problems and difficulties, sever you forever from the conditions of lack and limitation, and set you on the road to higher aspects of living life gloriously and serenely.

WHAT THE INFINITE POWERS OF THE MIND HAVE DONE FOR OTHERS

I have taught and written about the miracle-working powers of the mind for over thirty years, here and abroad. I have witnessed the following changes in the lives of countless numbers of people who sincerely used the Infinite Powers of their mind:

—Wealth in great abundance
—New friends and wonderful companions in life
—Protection from all danger
—Healing of so-called incurable maladies
—Freedom from self-condemnation and self-criticism
—Public acclaim, honor, and recognition
—New vitality and a zest for life
—Marital peace and happiness where discord was
—Serenity in this changing world
—And, above all, the joy of the answered prayer

This miracle-working power operates in all walks of life and at all levels

According to my observation and experience, the men, women, and teenagers who use this Power come from every level of society and from every possible income bracket. They are high school and college students, stenographers, taxi drivers, college professors, space scientists, chemists, pharmacists, bankers, medical doctors, chiropractors, housewives, telephone operators, motion picture directors, actresses, and truck drivers.

These people have discovered this mysterious but intensely real Power which picked them up from failure, misery, lack, and despair, and—in many instances "in the twinkling of an eye," as St. Paul said—It solved their problems, wiped away their tears, cut them free from emotional and financial entanglement, and placed them upon the great highroad to freedom from frustrating burdens and brought fame, fortune, glorious new opportunities for fulfilled living. Also, all these people discovered a magical healing love which healed their bruised and broken hearts and restored their souls for perfect living.

UNIQUE FEATURES OF THIS BOOK

The unique feature of this book is its down-to-earth practicality and every-day utility. You will learn to use your inborn extraordinary ability to visualize future events and to recognize the voice of intuition to guide you thereby for your greatest benefit.

How Infinite Mind reveals answers to you in dreams

The meaning of out-of-the-body experiences, travelling clairvoyance and what it means, how to make extrasensory perception work for you, and many other extraordinary powers of your mind are revealed to you in the following pages.

HOW TO LET WONDERS HAPPEN IN YOUR LIFE

The greatest working truths in life are the simplest. In this book, I have presented these great truths with the maximum of simplicity and dramatic clarity. This book will show how to let you rise above any problems you may have, and how to receive guidance and the blessings of the answered prayer.

Every day of your life will become richer, grander, nobler, and more wonderful as you follow the specific techniques presented in this book for releasing this Infinite Hidden Power within you for all good. Follow the instructions and tap this Infinite Power, and you will attract an abundance of all good things in life.

Begin now, with using this book, to release the imprisoned splendor within you, and *let* wonders of all that is good and satisfying happen in your life.

JOSEPH MURPHY

Contents

THE BENEFITS OF TRAVELING WITH GOD
  (*continued*)

ONE

How Infinite Power Can Give You an Exciting, Rich, New Life

This book is designed to teach you about the Infinite Power within you, which can lift you up from the midst of sickness, melancholia, failure, and frustration, and set you on the road to health, happiness, abundance, and security. I have seen miraculous transformations take place in men and women of all walks of life all over the world when they began contacting and releasing this Infinite Power within themselves.

Several months ago I spent two hours in a hospital talking with an alcoholic in the depths of despair. He began to use this Power and, as a result, is now strong, vital, and happy, and is operating a prosperous business. Like Paul in the Bible, he was changed in the "twinkling of an eye," and the Infinite Healing Power began to flow through him. His problems melted, peace came into his troubled mind, and he is back again with his wife and children.

This Infinite Power is positively, definitely, and absolutely waiting within you to be released. This Power is able to transform your life so completely, so radically, and so marvelously that after a few short weeks or months, it is possible that your close friends may not recognize you.

In this book you will read about a convicted criminal who had murdered several people and who is now a God-like man helping others to live life gloriously and peacefully. This man said to me, "A month after I started contacting this Infinite Power which you told me about, I looked at myself in the mirror and suddenly I realized I was not the same man. I can't repeat any of my former crimes." Then he added, "I'm beginning to wonder if I could have been that murderer." This man had discovered the Power within himself, which opens even prison doors, and it liberated him. The Infinite Healing Presence restored his soul. The Bible says, *He restoreth my soul* (Ps. 23:3).

This mysterious Infinite Power can cause miracles for you, too. As you peruse this and the following chapters, you will realize that you can direct the flow of this Power so that you can receive new ideas worth a fortune. All that is necessary is to have an open mind and a desire to lead a full, happy, exciting, and abundant life.

HOW THIS INFINITE POWER CAN WORK WONDERS IN YOUR LIFE

Why is it that some people are happy, successful, and prosperous, while others are poor and miserable? Why is it that some people are full of faith and confidence and live in the joyous expectancy of the best, acquiring riches and constantly rising on the ladder of success, while others are fearful, worried, depressed, and have become tragic failures in life? Why does one brother live in a beautiful mansion, while the other spends his life in a shabby tenement house unable to make ends meet?

The reason for the difference is that those who are leading exciting, adventurous, creative, and successful lives *have been making use of the Infinite Power that makes the difference.* For it is the use of this Mystic Power that brings to you all the vitality, prosperity, joy, and riches you need.

HOW YOU CAN USE THIS EXTRAORDINARY POWER

Through the ages men and women have been discovering an Infinite Power which revealed their hidden talents to them. They received inspiration from on High, and they also received marvelous and glorious original knowledge from the Infinite Storehouse within them. This Power can furnish you with the wisdom, power, and dynamics necessary to reach the goals selected by you. This book teaches you how to direct this Power for your betterment and welfare. All you have to do is to cooperate and align yourself with It.

You can use this Infinite Power to attract the right partner in business, find the right friends; it can provide you with the ideal home. You can prosper beyond your fondest dreams, and you can discover the joy and the freedom to be, and to do, and to travel as your heart desires.

WHY I WROTE THIS BOOK

To make this Primal Power which is the Power of God and the understanding of it available to all men and women is the reason I have written this book. It is your God-given birthright to contact and to use this power and to allow it to flow through your mind, body, business, and all your affairs so that you can rise triumphantly to the mental arena of dominion, joy and richer living.

What this wonder-working power has done for others

This book shows you how men and women of all walks of life have found Miraculous Healing for so-called incurable conditions, solutions to acute business problems, harmony in family relationships, methods by which to avert tragedies, and the use of clairaudience to save a man's life. These people have discovered how precognition made a fortune for a man, how tranquility and serenity replaced a mind in turmoil, how to attract the ideal Life Partner, how a mental movie attracted a million dollars, and how to turn failure into success.

This book has unique and extraordinary features

You will find all the necessary methods for using the Infinite Power within you in simple, usable techniques and formulas which you can readily apply in your everyday world. It not only answers questions, but gives solutions to personal problems, such as: How to gain confidence and poise, how to pray for success in business or a profession, how to use extrasensory perception to bless oneself and others, how to receive Divine guidance, how often to pray for a sick person, how to cooperate with the doctor, and how to pray effectively. This book tells why it is I have prayed and apparently received no answers, and how to pray for and recognize Divine guidance. Everything necessary for your instant use of the tremendous powers of the Infinite is here made perfectly clear and workable.

How you can start to live
a new fulfilled life

Everyone desires health, happiness, security, peace of mind, and true expression, but many say in their hearts, "It's too good to become true!" However, nothing is too good to be true, nothing too wonderful to last, for the Power, the Wisdom, and the Glory of God are the same yesterday, today, and forever, and are instantly available to all. It is within your power now to transform your whole life. Its simplicity is amazing and startling.

You will read in this book how a man turned a lifetime of failure into success at fifty. *You* can do the same. You will read how a woman of forty discovered the key to instant popularity and marriage. Let love work miracles for *you*, too.

HOW A BELLBOY DISCOVERED THE KEY TO
INSTANT PROMOTION

During my travels I spoke in Ottawa, Canada. After the talk, a young man chatted with me and told me that he had been a bellboy in New York City for two years and that a guest in the hotel had given him a paperback book entitled *The Power of Your Subconscious Mind.*[1] He read it four times and, following its directions, began to repeat prior to sleep, "Promotion is mine now. Success is mine now. Wealth is mine now." He lulled himself to sleep each night with these words, and at the end of about two weeks he was suddenly made Assistant Manager, and in six months General Manager, of a chain of hotels. He knew that the power

---

1 Joseph Murphy, *The Power of Your Subconscious Mind* (Englewood Cliffs, N.J.: Prentice-Hall, Inc., 1963) .

flowing through him was from God. "Just think," he said, "for several years of my life I was merely living on a trickle of the enormous potential within me." This man learned how to release the Infinite Power within him, and his whole life has been harmonized by this wondrous working power.

HOW A COLLEGE GIRL TURNED FAILURE INTO INSTANT SUCCESS

A few years ago, a young college girl came to see me at the request of her father. She was failing in college. I talked with her and found she had a good mind and a solid foundation of knowledge of the law of the mind. I asked her, "Why are you down on yourself? Why have such a low estimate of yourself?" She flushed considerably and said, "Oh, I'm the dumb one in the family. Father says that I'll never amount to much, that my brothers are smart, that they take after him, and that I'm stupid like my mother." "Well," I replied, "you are a child of God. All the infinite powers, attributes, qualities, and wisdom of God are within you waiting to be released and utilized. Tell your father from me that he should never make such frightfully negative statements to his daughter, but, rather, he should encourage you and remind you that the Infinite Intelligence of God is within you and when you call on It, It answers you. Tell him also that there are probably more of his genetic tendencies in you than those of your mother."

I gave her the following technique to be used every morning before she went to class and every night prior to sleep: "I am a child of God. I will never again underestimate my inner powers or demean myself in any way. I exalt God in the midst of me. I know God loves me and cares for me. It is written, . . . *He careth for you* (I Peter 5:7). Whatever I read and study is absorbed readily by my mind and it is reflected back to me instantaneously when I need it. I radiate love to my father and brothers and teachers and to my mother in the next dimension, where I know she is happy and free. Infinite Intelligence guides my studies and reveals to me everything I need to know at all times. I esteem myself, and I have a new estimate of myself, for I know the real Self of me is God. Any time I am prone to criticize or condemn myself, I will immediately affirm, 'God loves me and cares for me. I am His daughter.' "

She practiced this prayer process faithfully, and I am glad to report that she soon moved up in her grades and has since graduated from college *magna cum laude*. She discovered the Infinite Power for perfect living and began to release it. She ceased accepting the negative suggestions of her father and began to exalt God in the midst of her. Paul says, *Let every soul be subject unto the higher powers* (Romans 13:1). God is the only Presence and the only Power, and the powers that be are ordained of God.

HOW YOU CAN USE THE INFINITE POWER TO MAKE YOUR DREAMS COME TRUE

If you practice the principles of the Infinite Power for perfect living as portrayed and revealed in the following pages, you will see marvelous and fantastic changes for good taking place in your life. Your dreams, aspirations, ideas, and goals in life are thoughts, ideas, and mental pictures in your mind. You must realize that the idea or desire in your mind is as real as your hand or your heart. It has form, shape, and substance in another dimension of mind. Each chapter of this book will show you how to accept your desire, feel its reality, and know the Infinite Power within you will bring it to pass in Divine order. The Infinite Power which gives you the desire also will reveal to you the perfect plan for its unfoldment. All you have to do is to accept it and believe in it, and the Infinite Intelligence within you will bring it to pass.

HOW YOUR LIFE CAN BECOME AN EXCITING ADVENTURE

The miracle-working power of the Infinite existed before you and I were born, and before any church or even the world itself existed. The great eternal truths and principles of life which bless, heal, inspire, and elevate you antedate all religions. You and I are about to go forth on a journey into the inner recesses of our own mind, where we shall observe how it works, and learn of this wonderful, magical, healing, and transforming power that washes away all tears. We shall see how it binds up the wounds of the broken-hearted, proclaims liberty to the fear-ridden, disease-soaked mind, and liberates you completely from the self-imposed chains of poverty, failure, sickness, frustration, and limitations of all kinds.

All you need do is follow the simple but scientific methods outlined in the following chapters and then, *unite yourself,* mentally and emotionally with the good you wish to experience, and the Infinite Power will lead you to the fulfillment of your heart's desire.

This mental and spiritual journey on which you are now embarking will be the most wonderful "chapter" in your life—a healing and revealing experience. It will prove to be exciting, joyous, and the most rewarding of your life. Begin now, today. Let wonders and miracles happen in your life! Persist until day breaks and all the shadows disappear.

TWO

How to Set Up a Success Pattern for Richer Living

You were born to win and to triumph over all of the obstacles in life. God indwells you, and walks and talks within you. God is the Life-Principle within you. You are a channel of the Divine, and you are here to reproduce all the qualities, attributes, potencies, and aspects of God on the screen of space. That is how important and wonderful you are!

Whatever God starts, He finishes—whether it be a star, a cosmos, or a tree. In order to win and triumph in the game of life, join with the Cosmic Power within you, and as you align yourself in thought and feeling with this Infinite Power, you will find the Cosmic Power moving on your behalf and enabling you to achieve victory and the triumphant life.

HOW A NEW MENTAL PICTURE OF HIMSELF PAID RICH DIVIDENDS

"I have been with my firm for ten years and have not received a promotion or a raise in salary. There must be something wrong with me," a man, whom we shall call John, complained bitterly during his first consultation with me. While talking with him, I discovered that he had a subconscious pattern of failure guiding his affairs.

John was in the habit of downgrading himself constantly,

saying to himself, "I am no good, I am always passed over, I'm losing my job, there is a jinx following me." He was full of self-condemnation and self-criticism. I explained to him that these were two of the most destructive mental poisons he could generate, and that they would rob him of vitality, enthusiasm, energy and good judgment, ultimately leaving him a physical and mental wreck. Moreover, I elaborated further on his negative statements by pointing out that such statements as "I am no good, I am always passed over," were commands to his subconscious mind, which takes him literally, setting up blocks, delays, lack, limitation and impediments of all kinds in his life. The subconscious is like the soil, which takes all manner of seeds, both good and bad, and supplies nourishment for their development.

How John discovered the cause for failure within himself

He asked me, "Is this why I am passed over and ignored at our regular business conferences?" My answer was "Yes," because he had formed a mental picture of rejection and expected to be slighted and ignored. He was actually blocking his own good. John proved the age-old Biblical truth, *The thing which I greatly feared has come upon me* (Job 3:25).

How he practiced a realistic technique for success

This is how John extricated himself from the patterns of self-rejection, failure and frustration. I suggested to him that he dwell on this great truth: . . . *but this one thing I do, forgetting those things which are behind, and reaching forth unto those things which are before, I press toward the mark for the prize of the high calling of God.* . . . (Phil. 3:13,14).

He asked, "How can I forget the snubs, hurts and rebuffs? It is pretty hard." It can be done, but as I explained to him, he had to come to a clear-cut decision to drop the past and with positive determination to contemplate success, victory, achievement and promotion. Your subconscious knows when you mean what you say and will automatically remind you when, due to habit, you are prone to demean yourself, and you will immediately reverse the thought and affirm the good here and now.

He began to perceive the fallacy, as well as the foolishness, of carrying a mental load of disappointment and failures of the past into the future. It is like carrying a heavy iron bar on your shoulders all day long, thereby bringing about exhaustion and fatigue. Whenever a thought of self-criticism or self-condemnation came to his mind, he faithfully reversed it by affirming, "Success is mine, harmony is mine, and promotion is mine." After a while, the negative pattern was replaced by a constructive habit of thinking.

How John got to control his subconscious mind for success

I gave him the following simple technique to impregnate his subconscious mind. John was to begin to practice the art of picturing his wife congratulating him on his promotion while happily and enthusiastically embracing him. He made this mental picture very vivid and real by immobilizing his attention, relaxing his body, and focusing the lens of his mind on his wife. He would mentally converse with her as follows: "Honey, I received a terrific promotion today, the boss complimented me, and I will receive $5,000 a year more in salary! Isn't it wonderful?" He then imagined her response and heard the tone of her voice, saw her smile and gestures. All were real in his mind. Gradually, this mental movie moved by a sort of osmotic pressure from his conscious to his subconscious mind. A few days ago, John came in to see me and said, "I had to let you know. They have made me District Manager! That mental movie did the trick!"

John, having learned how his mind worked, began to realize that his habitual pattern of thinking, plus his mental movie, were penetrating the layers of his subsconscious mind and that the latter was being activated to attract all that he needed to bring his cherished desires to pass.

The working power of belief

The Bible says: *What things soever ye desire, when ye pray, believe that ye receive them, and ye shall have them* (Mark

11:24). This is simple language revealing to you that when you believe and live in the joyous expectancy of the best, you will receive the good you seek. John firmly believed that he would receive honor, recognition, promotion and a salary increase. According to his belief, was it done unto him.

John is a new man today and a happy one. He is buoyant and bubbling with enthusiasm. There is a light in his eye and a new emotional tone in his voice which indicates self-confidence and poise.

HOW A MENTAL PICTURE PRODUCED A MILLION DOLLARS

I had a conversation at the Palm Springs Spa Hotel with a man from San Pedro who told me that at forty, his life was one of disappointment, failure, depression and disillusionment. He had attended a lecture on "The Miracle of the Mind," given in San Pedro by the late Dr. Harry Gaze, world traveler and lecturer.

He said that after hearing that lecture he began to believe in himself and his inner powers. Always he had wanted to own and operate a movie theatre, but he had consistently failed at everything and had no money. He began with this affirmation: "I know I can succeed, and I will own and operate a theatre."

He told me that today he is worth $5 million and owns two theatres. He achieved success over supposedly insurmountable odds. His subconscious mind knew that he was sincere and that he meant to succeed. It knows your inner motivation and your real conviction. The Bible says: *Thou shalt decree a thing, and it shall be established unto thee . . .* (Job 22:28).

This man's magic formula for success was the mental picture he carried and to which he remained faithful, and his subconscious mind revealed to him everything necessary for the unfoldment of his dream.

HOW AN ACTRESS TRIUMPHED OVER FAILURE

A young actress came to see me, complaining bitterly about stage fright and panic during auditions and screen tests. She had failed, she said, to make the grade three times; she prolonged her doleful complaints into a lengthy jeremiad.

I discovered quickly that her real trouble was that she had a mental picture of panic before the camera, and like Job of old, she was dooming herself to failure: *The thing which I greatly feared is come upon me* . . . (Job 3:25).

How she gained confidence and poise

I taught this young actress the workings of her conscious and subconscious mind, and she began to realize that as she gave attention to constructive thoughts, she would automatically bring into her experience the benefits accruing from the thoughts dwelt upon. She devised a plan of her own for straight line thinking, knowing that there is a law of mind which responds to what you decree yourself to be, provided, of course, you believe what you claim to be true about yourself. For example, the more frequently you affirm to yourself, "I am afraid," the more fear you will generate. On the other hand, the more frequently you affirm, "I am full of faith and confidence," the more confidence and self-assurance you will develop.

I suggested she type thought-lifters on a card as follows:

"I am full of peace, poise, balance and equilibrium.
I fear no evil for God is with me.
I am always serene, calm, relaxed and at ease.
I am full of faith and confidence in the only power there is— God.
I am born to win, succeed and triumph.
I am successful in all my undertakings.
I am a marvelous actress and am immensely successful.
I am loving, harmonious, peaceful and feel my oneness with God."

She carried this "index card" with her. On trains, airplanes, and at frequent intervals during the day, she focused her mind on these truths. Actually, she committed them to memory after three or four days. As she reiterated these truths, they sank down into her subconscious mind and she discovered that these affirmations containing wonderful spiritual vibrations neutralized the noxious patterns of fear, doubt and inadequacy in her subconscious mind. She became poised, serene, calm and full of self-confidence. She had discovered the cosmic power for perfect living.

How her "mental movie" worked a miracle

She practiced the following technique for about five or six minutes morning, afternoon and night: She relaxed her body, sat quietly in a chair, and began to imagine that she was before the camera—poised, serene, calm and relaxed. She visualized herself as completely successful and imagined hearing congratulatory comments by the author and by her agent. She dramatized the role as only a good actress can, and made it very real and vivid. She realized that the Cosmic Power that moves the world also moves through the mental picture in her mind, compelling her to give marvelous renditions.

A few weeks later, her agent got another screen test for her, and she was so enthusiastic and exhilarated with the idea of triumph that she gave a wonderful performance. Today, with success following success, she is well on her way to becoming a great star.

YOU ARE RICH AND SUCCESSFUL BECAUSE OF WHAT YOU ARE INSIDE

I had an interesting conversation with a man at the Kona Inn on the island of Hawaii. He told me a fascinating story of his youth. He was born in London, England, and when he was very young his mother told him that he had been born into poverty, but that his cousin had been born into opulence and a vast fortune because this is the way God equalizes things. He said that later he discovered that what she had meant was that in a former life he had been very wealthy, and now God was getting even with him so that He sent him back to earth born into poverty in order to equalize justice.

"This," he said, "I looked upon as unmitigated balderdash; furthermore, I realized that the Cosmic Law is no respecter of persons, that God gives to all *according to their beliefs,* and that a man may be a multimillionaire possessing millions of English pounds sterling and be very illumined and spiritual at the same time. Some of the financially poor people, on the other hand, were most malevolent, selfish, envious and covetous."

During his youth this man sold papers in London and washed windows; he went to school at night, and worked his way through college; he is now one of the top surgeons in England. His motto in life is: "You go where your vision is." His vision was to become a surgeon, and his subconscious mind responded according to the mental image held in his conscious mind.

His cousin's father had been a multimillionaire and had given his son everything possible: private tutors, special educational trips to Europe, and he had sent him to Oxford University for five years. He provided his son with servants, automobiles, and all expenses. The cousin turned out to be a failure! He had been overindulged and had no confidence or self-reliance. He had no incentives, no obstacles to overcome, and no hurdles to rise above. He became an alcoholic and a rank failure in the art of living.

Which one was rich and which one was poor? The surgeon has overcome his handicaps. He said to me that he is thankful that he came up the hard way. "Justice is of the mind, and *if a man agrees with life for a penny a day, that is all he will receive.*" This man discovered that riches, success, achievement and prosperity are all of the mind, for as a man soweth in his subconscious mind so also shall he reap.

WHY YOU HAVE THE CHANCE OF A LIFETIME ALWAYS WITH YOU

Recently, a man said to me, "I had no chance in life. I was born into a poor family, and we never had enough to eat. I saw other boys in school whose fathers had lovely homes, private swimming pools, automobiles, and all the money they needed. Life is so unfair!"

I explained to him that often the hardship of poverty can be the goad to push you to the highest pinnacle of success. A beautiful home, a swimming pool, riches, prestige, success, a gold carriage, a Rolls Royce—all are ideas in the mind of man, which is one with the Infinite Mind of God.

Helen Keller's secret for
the good in her life

I explained to this man that the thinking of many people is wholly illogical, irrational, and most unscientific. For example, they say that Helen Keller's birth was an injustice, since she was deprived of her senses of sight and hearing in infancy. But she began to use the riches of the mind, and her blue eyes were enabled to "see," probably better than most people, the color of all the pageantry in opera; her deaf ears in a similar manner could "hear" the crescendos, diminuendos, and the full volume of orchestral music. She was perfectly aware of the clear notes of the lyric soprano, and she could grasp the humor of the play.

Helen Keller accomplished tremendous good in the world. Through meditation and prayer she awakened the inner eye and uplifted the minds and hearts of the deaf and the blind everywhere. She contributed faith, confidence, joy, and a tremendous spiritual uplift to thousands of shut-ins and others in the world. Indeed, she has accomplished much more than many people who have eyes and ears. She was not unfortunate or discriminated against by birth—There is no such thing as underprivileged or overprivileged.

THE MAGICAL KEY TO TURN FOR SUCCESS

The man was deeply moved by the story of Helen Keller, and I wrote for him the Cosmic plan for success, which he was to affirm fifteen minutes, three times a day: "I am in my true place in life, doing what I love to do, and am Divinely happy. I have a lovely home, a kind and wonderful wife, and a new and up-to-date car. I am giving of my talents to the world in a wonderful way, and God is revealing to me better ways in which I can serve humanity. I definitely and positively accept the fact that a new and wonderful opportunity is opening up for me. I know I am Divinely guided in all ways to my highest expression. I believe and accept abundance and security. I believe marvelous and wonderful opportunities are opening up for me now. I believe I am being prospered beyond my fondest dreams."

He had these affirmations typed on a card which he carried with him at all times, repeating these truths regularly and systematically for fifteen minutes, three times a day. When fear or anxiety came to his mind, he would pull the card out and reiterate these truths, knowing that the negative thoughts are always obliterated and dissipated by the higher constructive thoughts.

The power of belief in action

He realized that ideas are conveyed to the subconscious by repetition, belief, and expectancy, and the miracle-working power of his subconscious mind went to work on the impressions made upon it, as its nature is to respond according to man's habitual thinking.

Three months later all the things he meditated on came to pass. He is now married and has a lovely home, he has his own business which his wife bought for him, and he is doing what he loves to do and is Divinely happy. He has become a member of the Town Council and is contributing his services to the Boy Scouts of America and other worthwhile organizations. He had the chance of a lifetime—and so have you!

HOW A SALESMAN HELPED HIMSELF TO PROMOTION

A pharmaceutical salesman had not received a promotion in eight years; yet other co-workers apparently less qualified had been advanced to higher echelons of the business. His trouble was that he had a rejection complex.

My advice to him was to be nice to himself and to like himself more, because in reality the Self is God. I explained to him that he was the house where God dwelleth and that he should have a healthy, reverent, wholesome respect for the Divinity within him which created him, gave him life, and which equipped him with all the powers of the God-head. This would enable him to transcend all obstacles, to rise to affluence and perfect expression, and to acquire the capacity to lead a full and happy life.

This salesman quickly realized that he could use the same amount of mental energy to think constructive thoughts as destructive ones. He decided to stop thinking of reasons why he could not succeed, and he began to think of reasons why he could become a success. He practiced using the following mental and spiritual formula:

"From this moment forward, I place a new value on myself. I am conscious of my true worth. I am going to stop rejecting myself and definitely will never demean myself again. Whenever the thought of self-criticism comes to me, I will immediately affirm, 'I exalt God in the midst of me.' I respect and honor the Self of me which is God. I maintain a healthy, wholesome, reverent respect for the Infinite Power within me which is All-Wise and All-Knowing; It is the Ever-Living One, and the Self-Renewing Presence and Power. By day and by night, I am advancing, moving forward, and growing, spiritually, mentally, and financially."

This salesman set aside a certain period three times a day and identified himself with these truths, thereby gradually saturating his mind with poise, balance and equilibrium, plus a sense of his true values. As a result, after about three months, he became sales manager in the Midwest. In a recent note, he said, "I am on the way up, thanks to you."

The magic-mirror technique

In addition to the above mental and spiritual exercise, and in order to enable him to perceive the true sense of his own worth and importance in the scheme of life as a human being endowed with unique and extraordinary talents and abilities not yet released but dormant within him, I recommended that he practice the age-old mirror treatment. This is how he practiced it in his own words:

"Every morning after shaving, I looked into the mirror and said to myself boldly, feelingly and knowingly, 'Tom, you are absolutely outstanding, you are a tremendous success, you are full of faith and confidence and you are immensely wealthy. You are loving, harmonious and inspired.' I am one with God, and one with God is a majority. I am continuing this practice every morning. I am amazed at the many wonderful changes which have taken place in my business, finances, circle of friends, and in my home life. It has been two months since you gave me these two techniques of prayer and I have been promoted to sales manager in the Midwest."

This salesman identified himself with the truths he affirmed and established a new image of himself, thereby saturating his mind with poise, balance, equilibrium, prosperity and self-confidence. He believed implicitly in the response of his subconscious mind to his conscious mind activity, thereby discovering the majestic psychological truth of the Bible: *If thou canst believe, all things are possible to him that believeth* (Mark 9:23).

HOW AN OFFICE MANAGER OVERCAME PERSONALITY DEFECTS

During an interview, an office manager said to me that all the men and women in his office felt that he was too bossy, too critical, and too gloomy; there was a constant turnover in his office, and the general manager had complained about the number of resignations.

I explained to him that overexerting authority usually is a sign of lack of confidence; the person is trying to make himself feel self-reliant. A person can possess a quiet, orderly mind and never order others around in an arrogant manner, and yet be completely self-reliant; the noisy, loud-mouthed persons lack sincerity and inner balance.

At my suggestion he began to praise some of the employees for work well done, and he found that he would usually receive a corresponding friendly response, for by praising them he was building up their confidence in themselves. He ceased his constant criticism and carping attitude which marred the harmony of the office, and he also ceased the inner depreciation of himself which was in reality the cause of his trouble.

A secret technique for a better personality for success

In order to eradicate gloom, he began to practice deep breathing in conjunction with a specific affirmation. During inspiration he affirmed "I'm" and during expiration "cheerful." Through practice he was able to hold his breath a longer time between inspiration and expiration. He practiced this deep breathing fifty times and a hundred times until he got a deep subconscious response. Now he says he gets best results by thinking "I am cheerful" during inspiration and repeating it during expiration. He has proved the physiological value and sensation of well-being which routinely follows the drawing of deep breaths, which also favors impregnation of the subconscious mind with constructive ideas.

In addition, he practiced the following mental and spiritual prescription several times daily by affirming as follows: "From this moment forward, I cease all self-recrimination. I know there is nothing perfect in this universe, and I realize, also that all my employees and associates cannot possibly be perfect in all ways. I rejoice in their confidence, faith, cooperation, and interest in the work well done. I constantly identify with the good points in each of my associates.

"I am always confident in doing what I know well, and I gain confidence daily in other directions. I know that self-assurance and self-reliance are habits, and I can develop the wonderful habit of self-reliance just the same way as I recently gave up smoking. I supplant timidity with assurance, faith, and confidence in an Almighty Power which responds to my habitual thinking. I speak kindly to all my employees. I salute the Divinity within them, and I reiterate constantly, 'I can do all things through the Power of God which strengthens me.' When thoughts of self-criticism come to me, I supplant them immediately with this truth: 'I exalt God in the midst of me.' "

This office manager made it a practice to affirm these truths about six times slowly, quietly, and lovingly three times a day, knowing what he was doing and why he was doing it. He was building a new, constructive habit which displaced the old. At the end of six weeks, he was a transformed man, full of serenity and inner self-reliance. He promoted himself to Vice-President of the corporation with an income of $10,000 a year.

The Bible is right when it says: . . . *Be ye transformed by the renewing of your mind* . . . (Rom. 12:2) .

POINTS TO RECALL IN THIS CHAPTER

1. You were born to win and triumph over all obstacles through the Power of the Almighty within you, waiting to be stirred up and utilized by you.
2. Men and women who fail in their chosen work or profes-

sion usually have a mental pattern of failure. It is necessary to change the mental image, and to picture success, achievement, and the realization of your goal in life; then your subconscious mind will respond and compel you to achieve success because the law of your subconscious is compulsive.

3. Cease all self-condemnation and self-criticism. Forget the past and contemplate achievement, victory, triumph and success. You become what you contemplate.

4. When you are tempted to demean yourself, immediately reverse the thought and affirm your good here and now.

5. There is a law of mind which responds to what you decree yourself to be, provided, of course, you believe what you claim to be true about yourself. Ideas are conveyed to the subconscious by repetition, belief and expectancy.

6. Believe in yourself and your inner powers. Begin to affirm boldly: "I know I can succeed; I will accomplish what I want to achieve; I will be what I want to be; and I know my Deeper Mind will respond to my honest decision and conviction. I *know* the law of my subconscious never fails, and whatever I impress on it, it will likewise express and make manifest."

7. If suffering from stage fright, visualize yourself as successful, and imagine a loved one congratulating you on your wonderful success and poise.

8. You go where your vision is, regardless of whether you were born in the slums or in a palace. You are rich because of what you are *inside*. The Law is no respecter of persons; it is done unto you as you believe.

9. Helen Keller was deprived of the senses of sight and hearing in infancy, yet she accomplished wonders by an interior cosmic light.

10. A wonderful formula for success is to affirm with feeling: "God reveals to me better ways in which I can serve humanity."

11. Become conscious of your true worth. Realize *now* that you are a special and unique focal point for God's expression.

12. If you feel inferior or lack self-reliance, impress on your subconscious by habitually thinking: "I honor and exalt God in the midst of me. I maintain a wholesome, rever-

ent, and worshipful veneration for the Divinity within me." This attitude builds self-confidence and self-assurance.

13. Praise builds self-confidence among your employees or associates. Praise each one for the work well done, and realize that no one is perfect in this world. This attitude will banish the bossy and aggressive manner which is indicative of insecurity and self-demotion.

THREE

How to Achieve
Power and Control
over Your Life

I constantly receive letters from all over the country and from many foreign countries, and I find that most of the writers personally experience great vacillations of fate and fortune.

Many write and say something along these lines: "I get along fine for several months, in both health and finances, and then suddenly I find myself in the hospital or I meet with an accident or experience a great financial loss." Others say, "Sometimes I'm happy, joyous, vital, and bubbling over with enthusiasm, and suddenly an acute wave of depression seizes me. I can't understand it."

I have just finished interviewing a business executive who, some months ago, had reached what he termed the pinnacle of success and then, to use his own words, "the roof fell in" on him. He had lost his home, his wife had deserted him, and he had suffered a tremendous loss on the stock market.

He asked me, "Why did I rise so high and fall so suddenly? What am I doing wrong? How can I control these ups and downs?"

HOW THIS BUSY EXECUTIVE LEARNED TO
CONTROL HIS LIFE

This executive wanted to get away from these swings of fortune and health and to lead a balanced life. I explained to him that he could steer his life in the same manner as he steers his car to work every morning: The green lights say to go ahead; you can take your foot off the brake and step on the accelerator. You stop at the red lights, and, following the rules of the road, you arrive at your destination in Divine order.

I gave him the following spiritual formula with instructions to affirm these truths in the morning before entering his car, in the afternoon after lunch, and at night prior to sleep:

"I know that I can steer my thoughts and imagery. I am in control, and I can order my thoughts to give attention to what I desire. I know there is a Divine Power and Presence within me which I am now resurrecting and which responds to my mental call upon it. My mind is God's mind, and I am always reflecting Divine wisdom and Divine intelligence. My brain symbolizes my capacity to think wisely and spiritually. I am always poised, balanced, serene, and calm. God's ideas govern my mind and are in complete control; I no longer am subject to violent swings of mood, health, and wealth. My thoughts and words are always constructive and creative. When I pray, my words are full of life, love, and feeling; this makes my affirmations, thoughts, and words creative. Divine Intelligence operates through me and reveals to me what I need to know, and I am at peace."

The executive made a *habit* of using this prayer regularly and systematically, and as he continued to do so, gradually he reconditioned his mind to harmony, health, serenity, and poise. He no longer suffers from those changes in fortune of which he spoke, and he is leading a poised, balanced, and creative life.

The Bible says: *Thou wilt keep him in perfect peace, whose mind is stayed on thee: because he trusteth in thee* (Isa. 26:3) .

HOW A TEACHER CONQUERED HER FRUSTRATION

A teacher opened an interview with me with these remarks: "I'm in a rut. I feel frustrated; I have failed in love. I'm sick in mind and body. I am full of guilt, and I feel intellectually incompetent. Henry Thoreau was right when he said that the mass of men lead lives of quiet desperation!"

This young lady was quite attractive, well-read, very intelligent, and intellectually competent, but she was demeaning herself and was full of self-condemnation and self-criticism, all of which are deadly mental poisons and rob you of vitality, enthusiasm, and energy, and leave you a physical and mental wreck.

I explained to her that all of us have our ups and downs, our depressions, griefs, and illnesses, until we decide to control our lives and do our own constructive thinking. Otherwise, all of us will be subject to the mass mind which believes in sickness, accident, misfortune, and tragedies. Furthermore, we feel that we are subject to conditions and environments and that we are victims of our early training, indoctrination, and heredity.

The magic of giving up
frustrating thought habits

Our state of mind, and our beliefs, convictions, and conditioning control and determine our future. I explained to her that her present condition was due simply to the habitual force and authority of many thousands of thoughts, images, and feelings which she had consciously and unconsciously acquired and repeated through many years.

"Furthermore," I added, "you have said that you have traveled through Europe, the Orient, and North America several times, but you have not traveled anywhere *within yourself*. You are like the elevator man who says, 'I go up and down all day long, but I don't get anyplace in life.' You are repeating the same old patterns of thinking and idle wishing—the same routine procedures, plus constant mental agitation, turmoil, and grievances against your superiors, your pupils, and the school board."

How to travel mentally and
spiritually for self-renewal

She decided to make a definite change, to get out of the old routine, and to begin to experience the beauties, the satisfactions, and the glories of life. She affirmed the following truths several times daily, knowing that what she accepted consciously would find its way to her subconscious mind, and that by repetition she would recondition her mind to the success, happiness, and joy of life which she deserved to experience. The following spiritual medicine was imbibed by her through her eyes and ears several times daily:

"I am going to travel mentally and spiritually within myself and discover the treasure house of eternity within my depths. I am definitely and positively going to break the old routine. I am going to go to work by a different route every morning and will come home by a different way. I will no longer think according to the headlines of the newspapers or listen to gossip and negative thoughts about lack, limitation, disease, war and crime. I know that everything I do and experience in life is due to my thinking—conscious or unconscious. I realize that if I do not think for myself, the mass mind impinges on my subconscious mind and does my thinking for me, which is mostly negative and destructive.

"A revolution is now taking place in my mind, and I know that my life is transformed by the renewal of my mind. I immediately cease railing and mentally fighting conditions, as I know that this attitude actually magnifies my troubles. I now affirm and rejoice that I am an expression of God and that God hath need of me where I am, otherwise I would not be here. God is in action in my life, which means all-around harmony and serenity."

This repetitive prayer process worked wonders in the life of this college teacher. As she turned on the green light of constructive, confident thinking and became certain in the knowledge that all these mental seeds deposited in the subconscious would grow after their kind, love came into her life: she married the president of the college! She has received promotion in her profession, and she has had inner spiritual experiences, discovering that she had a great talent for painting, which has brought her endless joy. She is now releasing the imprisoned splendor within. Truly, prayer changes your life!

HOW A BUSINESSMAN SUCCESSFULLY REBUILT HIS BUSINESS

A pharmacist confided to me, "I am down in the depths! How can I go up the ladder? Thieves stole thousands of dollars of merchandise and money from my store, and my insurance covers only part of the loss. I have lost a small fortune in the stock market. How do you expect me to think constructive thoughts about that?"

"Well," I replied, "you can decide to think whatever you choose about anything. What you have lost has nothing to do with the way you decide to think about it. It is not what life does to you, it's the way you react to it."

I pointed out to this pharmacist that the thieves and the losses in the stock market did not and could not steal from him his nights and days, his health, the sun, the moon, or the stars, called the daily bread of the soul.

I also pointed out to him, "You are rich mentally and spiritually. You have a loving, kind, and understanding wife and two wonderful boys in college. No one can steal from you your knowledge of pharmacy, *materia medica,* pharmaceutical chemistry, or your business acumen and sagacity—all of these are riches of the mind.

"The thieves have not taken away from you your knowledge of the law of your subconscious mind or the way of the Infinite Spirit within you. It is foolish for you to dwell on the negatives. Chant the beauty of the good! It is now time for you to stir up the gift of God within you and to go forward in the light. Get in league with the universal Presence and Power which will restore to you manifold all the riches of life."

The Cosmic Law of action and reaction and how to use it

"Now," I said, "you know that you cannot gain or lose anything except through your mind; therefore, you will not admit the loss, but you will identify mentally and emotionally with the $30,000 you have lost, and whatever you mentally claim and feel to be true, your subconscious will honor, validate, and manifest for you. This is the law of action and reaction which is cosmic and universal."

Accordingly, he prayed as follows: "I am constantly on my guard against negative thinking, and I cast it out of my mind whenever it tends to enter in. I have faith in the Infinite Power and Presence that always works for good. My faith is in the goodness and guidance of the Infinite God. I open my mind and heart to the influx of the Divine Spirit, and I discover an ever increasing sense of power, wisdom, and understanding.

"I am mentally and emotionally identified with the $30,000, and I know that I cannot lose anything except I accept the loss—

which I positively, definitely, and absolutely refuse to accept. I know the way my subconscious works. It always magnifies what I deposit in it; therefore, the money comes back to me pressed down, shaken together, and running over.

"I know that I will no longer experience the ups and downs of life, but that I will lead a dynamic, creative, balanced, and purposeful life. I know that prayer is the contemplation of the truths of God from the highest standpoint. I know that the thoughts and ideas I habitually dwell upon become dominant in my mind, and they rule, govern, and control all my experiences. My family, my store, and all my investments are watched over by the Overshadowing Presence of God, and the whole armor of God surrounds me, enfolds me, and enwraps me. I bear a charmed life. I know that eternal vigilance is the price of peace, harmony, success, and prosperity. With mine eyes stayed on God, there is no evil on my pathway."

The pharmacist made a habit of reiterating and affirming these eternal verities. After some weeks had passed, his broker called him and gleefully informed him that he had recuperated all his losses due to a rebound on the stock market. Furthermore, he received a wonderful offer for a piece of land he had held for ten years; he sold it for $60,000, his original investment in the land being $5,000.

He has discovered the wonderful workings of his mind and realizes he does not have to suffer from the ups and downs of life.

THE MASS MIND AND HOW TO OVERCOME ITS NEGATIVE EFFECTS ON YOU

The *mass mind* simply means the mind operating in three billion people in this world. All of them are thinking into the one universal mind, and it does not take much stretch of the imagination to realize the kind of imagery, feelings, beliefs, superstitions, and ugly, negative thoughts impressed on that universal mind.

It is also true that millions of people throughout the world are pouring into the mass mind—sometimes referred to as the race mind—thoughts of love, faith, confidence, joy, goodwill, and success, plus feelings of triumph, accomplishment, and victory over problems and an emanation of peace and goodwill to all men. However, they are still in the vast minority, and the dominant feature of the mass mind is one of negativity.

The mass mind believes in accidents, sickness, misfortune, wars, crimes, disasters, and catastrophes of all kinds. The mass mind is rampant with fear, and the children of fear are hate, ill will, resentment, hostility, anger, and disease.

It is, therefore, very simple for anyone who wants to think at all to realize that he will be subject to trials and tribulations of all kinds until he learns to pray scientifically—and to keep up his armor of protection. All of us are subject to the influence of the mass mind, the spell of negativity, the sway and power of propaganda, and the opinions of others. And, as long as we refuse to become "straight-line" thinkers, we shall experience the violent swings of fortune and misfortune, sickness and health, wealth and poverty. If we refuse to think for ourselves from the standpoint of the eternal principles and truths of God, we will be only one of the mass and will inevitably experience the extremes of life.

HOW TO NEUTRALIZE NEGATIVE INFLUENCES
OF THE MASS MIND

Take complete control of your mind by constructive thinking and visioning, and then you will neutralize the negative suggestion of the mass mind which is forever attacking the minds of all of us. You can rise above the negative mass mind. The Bible says in John 12:32: *I, if I be lifted up . . . draw all men unto me;* i.e., if you elevate your mind by identifying with the principles of harmony, health, peace, joy, wholeness, health, and perfection, *and make a habit of doing so,* by the law of attraction you will attract into your life and experience those qualities and attributes of God.

The following is an excellent prayer which will enable you to rise above the mass mind and to establish an immunity to the false beliefs and fears of the race:

"God is, and His Presence flows through me as harmony, health, peace, joy, wholeness, beauty, and perfection. God thinks, speaks, and acts through me. I am Divinely led in all my ways. Divine right action governs me. Divine law and order govern my entire life. I am always surrounded by the sacred circle of God's eternal love, and the healing light of God surrounds and enfolds me. Whenever my thoughts wander away in fear, doubt, or worry, I know it is the mass mind thinking in me. Immediately, I boldly affirm, 'My thoughts are God's thoughts, and God's power is with my thoughts of good.' "

Continue to identify with and to meditate on the above prayer and you will rise above the discord, confusion, and extremes and tragedies of life. You will no longer experience the ups and downs, but rather, you will enjoy a constructive, vital, and active life full of creativity and the rhythm of life.

HOW TO GET IN TUNE WITH THE INFINITE

Some months ago, a woman from North Carolina wrote me, saying that the world is going to the dogs, that our morals are at a low ebb, that corruption is rampant, and that teenage violence, crime, and scandal are the news of the day. Then she added, "We may be annihilated by an atomic bomb any day. How do we tune in on God in the midst of all this degeneracy, pornography, and the cesspool of iniquity in which we find ourselves?"

I answered her along these lines and admitted that what she mentioned was true, but that the Bible says, . . . *Come out from among them, and be separate* (II Cor. 6:17). She must have the ability and capacity to rise above the world negation and to lead a full and happy life right where she is. I pointed out to her that all she had to do was to look around and she would find thousands of people who are happy, vital, joyous, and free, leading constructive lives, and contributing to humanity in countless ways.

We have witnessed the extremes of the Victorian period with all its sexual taboos and restrictions, and these repressions caused people to move to the opposite extreme that we are experiencing today in the immorality and lewdness prevalent in various parts of the world.

Nature works by extremes. History witnessed the "sweat shops," where people—even children—worked under indescribable conditions and were inadequately paid, housed, and fed; actually, it was a sort of serfdom. Now there has been a swing to the opposite in England, the United States, and in other countries, where some unions have become so tyrannical that they have even closed down the transportation systems of a whole city.

The ancient Hebrew wisdom says: "Change eternal is at the root of all things." You must find an anchor within you to tie to and make a Divine adjustment. Tune in to the Infinite Power within you and let this Presence guide, direct, and govern you in all your ways. You can enthrone Divine wisdom in your conscious mind by claiming that the wisdom of God anoints your intellect and is a lamp unto your feet and a light on your path. Following is a prayer I gave to the troubled woman in North Carolina:

The prayer that changed a life— and can change yours

"I realize that I cannot change the world, but I know I can change myself. The world is an aggregation of individuals, and I know that people who are ruled by the mass mind, propaganda, and sense opinions are subject to the tragedies, sorrows, accidents, illnesses, and failures in life until they learn to control their minds with Divine ideas which heal, bless, inspire, elevate, and dignify their souls. I realize that the mass of people are under the sway of the mass mind, full of errors, false beliefs, and negation of all kinds.

"From this moment forward, I no longer fight conditions or situations, and I cease rebelling at news of subversives, immorality, and corruption in high places. I write constructive letters to congressmen, senators, movie producers, and newspapers, and I pray for right action, beauty, harmony, and peace for all people everywhere. I am in tune with the Infinite, and Divine law and order govern my life. I am Divinely guided and inspired. Divine love fills my soul, and waves of light, love, truth, and beauty go forth as a mighty wave of spiritual vibration which tends to lift all men up, for it is said, *I, if I be lifted up, will draw all men unto me*" (John 12:32) .

A happy outcome of this prayer

This young lady recently phoned me and said, "Your letter was the greatest eye-opener I have ever read. I'm on 'cloud nine'! Now

I know that there is no one to change but myself. Being in tune with the Infinite, I am in tune with the Presence of God in the hearts of all men and women in the world!"

The Bible says: *Great peace have they who love thy law, and nothing shall offend them* (Ps. 119:165).

POINTS TO RECALL IN THIS CHAPTER

1. You can steer your thoughts, images, emotions, and reactions to life just as easily as you can steer your car in the right direction.
2. You can order your thoughts and make them give attention to the desires, goals, and objectives in your life. You are the master, and you mold, fashion, and create your own destiny.
3. When you pray, let your words be full of life, love, and feeling; this makes your affirmations creative.
4. All of us will have our swings of fortune until we decide to take control of our lives and do our constructive thinking along God-like ways; otherwise, we will be subject to the mass mind which believes in all manner of sickness, accidents, tragedies, and misfortune.
5. Many people travel all over the world but go nowhere within themselves. Travel within mentally and spiritually, and you will discover in your depths the riches of Heaven.
6. Everything you do and experience in life is due to your conscious and subconscious thinking. Think good and good follows.
7. You can decide to think whatever you choose about anything. What you have lost or suffered has nothing to do with the way you decide to think about it.
8. You cannot lose anything except you admit the loss in your mind. Mentally and emotionally identify with money you have lost and your subconscious will respond and multiply it in your experience.
9. The "mass mind" means the mind operating in three billion people on this planet. It is composed of good and bad thoughts, but the dominant phase of the mass mind is negative—it is the mind full of the fears, doubts, superstitions, hates, jealousies, greed, and lust of millions of people.

10. You can rise triumphantly over the world negation and lead a full and happy life by enthroning in your mind ideas which heal, bless, inspire, elevate, and dignify your soul.

11. Tune in with the Infinite and feel and know that the Infinite Power and Presence governs, controls, and directs your life, and you will lead a balanced and creative life free from the great swings of fate.

12. You can lift yourself up above all the servitude and bondage of the mass mind by exalting God in your midst and realizing that God's love fills your soul and His wisdom anoints your intellect.

FOUR

How You Can Unleash Infinite Power to Benefit Every Phase of Your Life

During my lecture tours, I once addressed a group of people in the mountains of Colorado. In the course of a conversation later at a luncheon, my host said that most people worry too much and thus deprive themselves of a full and happy life.

He told me of an elderly man who had lived in one of the cabins in the mountains nearby. The neighbors felt sorry for him, because he always seemed to be tired, depressed, worried and lonesome. He wore tattered clothes and possessed an old automobile of 1928 vintage. He seemed to have nothing to live for, and he apparently had no relatives or friends. Occasionally he went to the grocery store and invariably asked for stale bread and the most inexpensive food, and he usually paid for it in frugally doled out pennies and nickels.

Eventually when he did not appear for a couple of weeks, the neighbors went to his shack and found that he had died. The sheriff searched the old cabin for names of relatives or a clue to his real identity. To everyone's amazement, they found that the poor old man had more than $100,000 in bundles of $25. He evidently had made much money in his earlier years and had never invested it or deposited it in banks.

He had acquired considerable money, but he had failed to use it

33

to lead the rich life or to spend it for an altruistic purpose. Further, he failed to invest it wisely for interest and dividends. My host said that it was fear that had dominated the old man. He had worried lest people might learn of his money and steal it from him. He had been a very negative thinker, yet he had had a fortune within and without to share in the good life. He *could* have had much enjoyment and happiness.

YOU HAVE A FORTUNE TO SHARE

The treasure house of infinity is within you. You have the key which unlocks the storehouse of all kinds of treasures. The key is your thought, which will bring you far more wealth of every description than that lonely and fearful old man had—and much more of everything you want!

You have the key to the most wonderful and marvelous power in the world—the power of the Infinite within you. The Bible says, . . . *Behold, the kingdom of God is within you* (Luke 17:21). Seek first the knowledge and awareness of this inner Presence and Power, and all things that you want shall be added unto you.

Remember, *your* powers are the powers of the God-head, which the average person habitually and through ignorance fails to use. You have a fortune to share by stirring up the gift of God within you. You can share the gifts of love and goodwill with others; you can share a smile and a cheerful greeting; you can give compliments and appreciation to your co-workers and employees; you can share creative ideas and the love of God with all those around you.

You can see the intelligence and the wisdom of God in your sons and daughters and call it forth knowingly and feelingly, and what you claim and feel will be resurrected in their lives. You can have a new idea worth a fortune which you can share with the world— perhaps a sonata, an invention, a play, a book, or a creative and expansive idea in your business or profession which will bless yourself and others.

Remember that the only chance you have is the one you make for yourself. You have the chance of a lifetime! Begin now to

mentally tap the infinite reservoir within you, and you will find
yourself moving onward, upward, and Godward.

HOW YOU CAN RISE TO THE HEIGHTS
OF YOUR DESIRES

Some years ago, during a lecture Mrs. Vera Radcliffe, our
church organist in Los Angeles, told the stirring drama of
Paderewski's trials and tribulations before he became world-
famous. He had been advised by the famous composers and authorities on music in his day that he had no possible future as a
pianist, and that he should forget about it! The professors at the
Warsaw Conservatory, where he went to study, tried their best to
discourage his desire. They pointed out that his fingers were not
well-formed and that he should try writing music instead.

Paderewski rejected their negative pronouncements and identified himself with his inner powers; he subjectively realized that he
had a fortune to share with men throughout the world, namely,
the melody of God and the music of the spheres.

He practiced arduously and diligently for hours every day. Pain
tortured him in thousands of his concerts, and, as Mrs. Radcliffe
said, blood occasionally oozed from his injured hands. He persevered, however, and his "stick-to-itiveness" paid fabulous dividends. The inner powers responded to his call and to his effort. *He
knew that the key to his triumph was his contact with the Divine
Power within him.*

As time went on, Ignace Paderewski's musical genius was
acknowledged all over the world, and men of all walks of life paid
homage to this man who touched and sensed his oneness with the
Great Musician within—the Supreme Architect of the universe
itself.

Paderewski's secret of success

Like Paderewski, you too have the power to reject completely
the negative suggestions of those in authority who tell you that
you cannot be what you want to be. Realize, as did Paderewski,
that the God-Presence which gave you the desire and the talent is

the same Power that will open up the door and reveal the perfect plan for the fulfillment of your dream.

Trust the Divine Power within you, and you will find that this inner Presence and Power will lift you up, heal you, inspire you, and set you on the high road to happiness, serenity, and the fruition of your ideals.

HOW TO COPE WITH SEEMING WORLDLY INJUSTICE

During a visit to Hawaii, a junior executive said to me, "There is no justice in the world. Everything is so unfair. Corporations are soulless; they have no heart. I work hard and spend long hours after closing time, but men under me are promoted and I am passed up. It's all so unfair and unjust."

My explanation was the cure for this man's wrath. I acknowledged that there is injustice in the world and that, as Robert Burns said, "man's inhumanity to man makes countless thousands mourn," but that the law of the subconscious mind[1] is impersonal and eminently fair at all times.

Your subconscious mind accepts the impress of your thought and reacts accordingly. It's the set of the sails, and not the gales, that determines the way you go. It is your inner thought, feeling, and imagery—in other words, your mental attitude—operating within you, rather than the winds of negative thoughts and the waves of fear from without, that makes the difference between promotion and success, and failure and loss. The law is absolutely just and mathematically accurate, and your experiences are the exact reproduction of your habitual thinking and imagery.

I briefly explained to the young executive the familiar story of the laborers in the vineyard, where all the workmen received a penny. Even those who came in at the eleventh hour received the same wages as those who worked all day long; also the men who came in at the third hour, the sixth hour, and the ninth hour received the same wages. When they saw that the men who had worked but one hour got the same wages, they were jealous and angry, but the answer they received was this: *Didst not thou agree with me for a penny?* (Matt. 20:13) .

---

[1] Joseph Murphy, *The Power of Your Subconscious Mind* (Englewood Cliffs, N.J.: Prentice-Hall, Inc., 1963) .

The law is plainly stated in Matt. 18:19: . . . *If two of you shall agree on earth as touching any thing that they shall ask, it shall be done for them of my Father which is in heaven.* This means that when your conscious and subconscious mind agree on promotion, success, abundance, and right action, the law of your subconscious mind will honor, execute, and bring it to fruition in your experience.

I added, "You are resentful, angry, and full of condemnation and criticism of the organization which employs you. These negative suggestions enter your subconscious and have resulted in loss of promotion, financial increase, and prestige."

A specific program and formula for daily use

I gave him the following mental and spiritual formula to practice daily:

"I know that the laws of my mind are absolutely just, and that whatever I impress on my subconscious mind is reproduced mathematically and accurately in my physical world and circumstances. I know that I am using a principle of mind, and a principle is absolutely impersonal. I am equal before the laws of mind, which means it is done unto me as I believe. I know that justice means fairness, rightfulness, and impartiality, and I know that my subconscious is absolutely impersonal and impartial.

"I realize that I have been angry, resentful, and jealous, and that I have also demeaned, criticized, and condemned myself. I have psychically persecuted, assailed, and tortured myself, and I know that the law is 'as within, so without'; therefore, my boss and associates attest to and confirm objectively what I have thought and felt subjectively.

"What I accept completely in my mind, I will get in my experience, regardless of conditions, circumstances, or the powers that be. I wish success, prosperity, and promotion for all my associates, and I exude goodwill and blessings to all people everywhere. Promotion is mine; success is mine; right action is mine; wealth is mine. As I affirm these truths, I know they are deposited in my subconscious mind—the creative medium—and wonders are happening in my life.

"Every night of my life, prior to sleep, I imagine my wife congratulating me on my wonderful promotion. I feel the reality of all this, mentally and emotionally. My eyes are closed and I am drowsy, sleepy, and in a passive, receptive state of mind, but I hear her congratulatory words, feel her embrace, and see her gestures. The whole mental movie is vivid and realistic, and I go off to sleep in this mood, knowing that *God giveth his beloved in sleep*" (Ps. 127:2).

This executive discovered that the law of his mind established justice (conformity to the principles of his mind). Having enthroned right thoughts, right imagery, and right feeling in his conscious mind, his subconscious responded accordingly. This is the equity of the mind. The laws of your mind are the same yesterday, today, and forever. At the end of a few months following this prayer process, this executive has been voted president of his corporation and is prospering beyond his fondest dreams.

HOW A WOMAN SHARED HER FORTUNE AND GOT RICHER

A few years ago, I had many interesting talks with a Canadian woman. She informed me that she looks upon money and wealth like the air that she breathes. She felt as free as the wind. Ever since she was a child, this woman had claimed: "I am rich; I am God's daughter; God gave me richly all things to enjoy." This was her daily prayer.

She has accumulated millions of dollars and has endowed colleges and universities, establishing scholarships for worthy boys and girls, and has established hospitals and nurses' training centers in remote parts of the world. Her joy is in giving wisely, judiciously, and constructively, and she got richer than before.

Why the rich get richer and the poor get poorer

She said to me one day, "You know, the old aphorism is absolutely true: 'The rich get richer and the poor get poorer.' To those people who live in the consciousness of affluence and abundance, wealth flows by the cosmic law of attraction. Those who expect

poverty, privation, and lack of all kinds are living in the consciousness of poverty, and by the law of their own mind they
attract more lack, misery, and deprivation of all kinds."

What she said is definitely true. Many people who are living in
poor circumstances are envious and resentful of the wealth of their
neighbors; this mental attitude results in even more lack, limitation, and poverty in their lives. They are, probably unwittingly,
blocking their own good. Yet they have a fortune to share if they
would but open their minds to the truth of being and realize that
they, too, have the key which unlocks the treasure house or gold
mine within.

The following illustration shows how any man has a fortune to
share.

HIS FORTUNE WAS WHERE HE WAS—
BUT HE WAS BLIND TO IT

A friend of mine, who lived in Northern Alaska, once wrote me
and said that life was unbearable. He felt that he had made a
tragic mistake in going to Alaska to seek his fortune, that his
marriage was a complete failure, that prices were exorbitant, and
that cheating and over-charging were rampant. When he had gone
to court to dissolve his marriage, the judge was crooked and he got
a raw deal. He concluded by saying that there is no justice in this
world.

What he said was true enough. All we need do is read the
morning newspaper in any metropolitan area, and we read of
murder, crime, purse snatching, mugging, rape, malfeasance and
misfeasance in office, corruption in high places, and venality on
the bench and in the legislative chambers—but we must remember
that all of these are man-made, and you can *come out from among
them and be separate* (II Cor. 6:17).

You can rise above the mass mind, man's cruelties, and greed, by
aligning yourself with the principle of right action and absolute
justice within you. God is absolute justice, absolute harmony, all
bliss, boundless love, fullness of joy, absolute order, indescribable
beauty, absolute wisdom, and supreme power. All of these are
attributes, qualities, and potencies of God. When you dwell on
these qualities and contemplate the truths of God, you rise above

the injustice and the cruelties of the world and you build a conviction counter to all its false beliefs and erroneous concepts.

In other words, you build up a Divine immunity—a sort of
spiritual antibody—to the mass mind.

This explanation was a prelude to my direct reply to my friend.
I wrote to him, suggesting that he stay where he was and that I
suspected he wished to run away from his responsibilities and was
merely seeking an escape. I wrote a short prayer, as follows:

"Where I am, God is. God indwells me, and God has need of me
where I am now. This God-Presence within me is infinite intelligence and all-wise, and reveals to me the next step, opening up for
me the treasures of life. I give thanks for the answer, which comes
to me as an intuitive feeling or an idea which wells up spontane-
ously from my mind."

He followed my advice and was eventually reconciled with his
wife. He bought a camera and took pictures of Northern Canada
and Alaska, wrote short stories, and amassed what he considered a
small fortune. A year passed and for a Christmas present he sent
me $2,000, suggesting that I take a vacation in Europe, which I
did.

This man had found happiness by tapping the treasure house
within, and he discovered that his fortune was right where he
was.

HOW A PROFESSOR DISCOVERED A FORTUNE

Recently I talked with a college professor who was very angry
over the fact that his brother, a truck driver, was earning $15,000
and he was receiving only $8,000 a year. He said, "It is all so
unfair. We must change the system. I worked hard and toiled for
six years to get my Ph.D. degree, and my brother never even went
to high school!"

This professor was brilliant in his particular field, but he was
unaware of the laws of mind. I told him that a waitress in my
favorite restaurant earns more than $300.00 a week with tips and
indicated that these disparities of which he spoke are everywhere.

I explained to the professor that he could rise above the mass
mind, sometimes referred to as the race mind or as the law of
averages, i.e., the five-sense mind, the mind that thinks from the
standpoint of circumstance, conditions, and traditions.

Accordingly at my suggestion he began to practice the "mirror treatment" every morning, which consisted of standing before the mirror and affirming: "Wealth is mine. Success is mine. Promotion is mine now." He continued affirming these statements for about five minutes every morning, knowing that these ideas would impregnate his subconscious mind.

Gradually, he began to feel the way he would feel were all these conditions true, and at the end of one month's time he received an offer from another university at $13,000 a year. Suddenly he discovered a flair for writing, and his manuscript has been accepted by a large publishing house, which will bring him a sizable income.

The professor discovered that he was not a victim of "the system" or the scheduled salary scale outlined by the university. His fortune lay in his discovery of the hidden power within him.

HOW A SECRETARY'S FAITH WORKED WONDERS FOR HER

A legal secretary complained to me as follows: "I never get the breaks. The boss and the other girls in the office are mean and cruel to me. I have been mistreated at home and by my relatives all my life. There must be some kind of a jinx following me. I'm no good. I should jump in the lake!"

I explained to her that she was mentally cruel to herself, and that her self-flagellation and self-pity must have substantiation and confirmation on the external plane of life. In other words, the attitudes and actions of those around her attested to and conformed with her inner state of mind.

She thereupon immediately ceased punishing herself and learned that *faith without works is dead* (Jas. 2:17). What is faith? *Faith is the substance . . . of things not seen* (Heb. 11:1). Faith is the mental image which in time clothes itself in a body of manifestation. Every mental image sustained is bound to work itself out.

This secretary, at my behest, pictured herself being congratulated by her employer for very efficient work, and she also imaged him announcing an increase in salary for her. She constantly diffused love and goodwill to her employer and to all her associates.

Having faithfully sustained her mental image many times a day for several weeks, she was completely dumbfounded when her employer not only congratulated her on her work, but furthermore asked her to marry him! In a few hours' time, as I finish this chapter, I will have the pleasure of being the officiating clergyman.

She has found the key which unlocked the treasure house. Her faith proved to be *the substance of things hoped for and the evidence of things not seen* (Heb. 11:1).

POINTS TO RECALL IN THIS CHAPTER

1. Your fortune begins with *you*. Your thought and your feeling create your destiny. All the powers, attributes, and potencies of God are locked in your subconscious mind, and you have the key which unlocks the treasures within, namely, your *thought*.
2. There is a hidden power within you that can lift you up from a sick bed, heal you, and set you on the road to happiness, serenity, and all the blessings of life.
3. You can draw forth from your subconscious mind an idea worth a fortune. Call on the Infinite Intelligence within you for creative ideas, and you will receive them. Ask and you shall receive.
4. By perseverance, endurance, and determination to reach the top, you can rise to the heights of your profession or ideal in life. Set your sights high! You have the power to completely reject the negative statements of others and to trust the Supreme Power within you which never fails.
5. It is the set of the sails and not the gales that determines your fortune. It is your inner thought, feeling, and imagery that determine your future and bring you the riches of life. This is the justice of the mind. Forget the inequities and injustices of the world or mass mind.
6. If you agree with life "for a penny a day," life responds accordingly.
7. Whatever you impress on your subconscious—good or bad —will appear as form, function, experience, and events in your life.
8. Realize that God gave you richly all things to enjoy.

Claim these gifts and riches will flow into your life. The
the more you give the more you will receive.

9. Your fortune is right where you are. You can rise above
   all the lack and limitation of the world, if you will mentally and emotionally unite with the good things you
   want; your subconscious will respond accordingly.

10. If you want to make more money and to enjoy the rich
    and abundant life, stop comparing yourself with others
    and being envious of their wealth or success.

11. Your faith is the confident expectancy that the mental
    image you sustain in your mind will be manifested.

FIVE

How to Foresee the Future and Recognize the Voice of Intuition

One of the most perplexing faculties of the human mind is that of *prevision* or the ability to perceive a future event before it happens on the objective or material plane of life. Occasionally, I have had an advance glimpse of events that have occurred days, weeks, and sometimes even months afterwards.

For example, in January of 1967, a minister friend of mine visited me and suggested that I arrange a lecture tour with him to the Holy Land in May. I told him that I would think about it and let him know.

I spoke to my subconscious mind that night prior to sleep and affirmed as follows: "Infinite Intelligence within my subconscious mind is All-Wise and reveals to me the right decision regarding the proposed trip to Israel, Jordan, etc."

That particular night, I had a vivid dream in which I saw the war headlines in both the *Los Angeles Times* and the *Citizen-News*. In the dream state, I also witnessed a violent tank and air battle between the Israelis and the Arabs. I witnessed a vivid realization of things to come, apparently five months later. On awakening from the dream state I telephoned my friend and told him of the contents of my dream, and, strange to say, he had had a similar dream! He also had prayed for Divine guidance.

Both of us thereupon dismissed the idea of conducting the lecture tour in the Holy Land. Subsequent events—the tragedy of the Arab-Israeli war—proved the truth of the inner vision.

The Bible says: *Trust in the Lord* (the Law of your subconscious mind), *and do good; so shalt thou dwell in the land, and verily thou shalt be fed* (Ps. 37:3).

YOUR FUTURE IS IN YOUR MIND NOW

Your mind is full of thoughts, beliefs, opinions, convictions, impressions, and sundry concepts—both good and bad. The Cosmic Law of mind is that whatever we mentally accept and believe will be made manifest and concrete in our lives.

If it were possible for you to photograph in some manner the contents of the subconscious minds of your friends, you could accurately foretell their futures and determine the events that are going to happen to each one of them. Dr. Rhine of Duke University has given ample proof of extrasensory perception, such as clairvoyance, precognition, clairaudience, retrocognition, and telekinesis in countless experiments, all of which have been documented.

A highly intuitive person, a good psychic, or a mediumistic clairvoyant could perceive the contents of your subconscious and clearly see (clairvoyance) the experiences and events, both good and bad, which you are about to meet on the screen of space. The reason for this is that your thoughts, beliefs, plans, and purposes, and their manifestation are completed in mind, just the same as is the idea of a new building in the mind of the architect, and they may be accurately viewed by a good clairvoyant.

To elaborate a little further, I should like to state that it is possible for an intuitive person, in a perceptive, passive, and subjective state of mind, to tap the contents of the subconscious mind of another person and reveal the same to the conscious mind or waking self of that man. In other words, in a passive, semi-trance state, a sensitive or highly psychic person tunes in with the decisions, plans, ideas, fears, phobias, fixations, and desirable states, and the subjective acceptance of marriage, divorce, business ventures, trips, and various other impressions, in the *other person*.

The psychic or medium who is tuning in with your subjective feelings, beliefs, and impressions translates all these in his or her own terminology and predicts accordingly. Often the psychic or clairvoyant is extraordinarily accurate—not always 100 per cent, but sometimes close to it.

You must remember that what the medium sees or feels must be filtered through and tinctured by the contents of his own mentality, and for that reason it comes out somewhat differently with each medium or psychic. This is why you sometimes receive different readings or interpretations from different psychic readers.

HOW PRECOGNITION SAVED A FORTUNE AND MADE A NEW ONE

I am friendly with a prominent real estate operator who told me that every night of his life before retiring he has meditated on the 91st Psalm and has claimed Divine guidance, protection, and right action in all his activities. One night, early in 1966, following a vivid prophetic dream in which he saw the headlines of a local newspaper announcing a big drop in the market, he had an intense, overpowering urge to sell all his blue chip stocks, in which he had invested $400,000; he said it was like an inner voice commanding him, and it was persistent.

He followed this intuitive urge and sold out the next day before the market closed. The following day there was a big drop, and his blue chip stocks have not yet returned to their former highs, some having dropped 20 and 30 points. His savings were extensive. He has since repurchased many of these stocks at a much lower price and has thus made another small fortune.

His remark was, "I saved a fortune and I made a fortune." He saw the event before it happened and he listened to the voice of his intuition. Intuition means "taught from within."

HOW A MOTHER'S PREVISION SAVED HER SON'S LIFE

I interviewed an overwrought, emotion-wracked mother whose son was an Air Force pilot in Vietnam. She had been suffering from a recurrent dream which distressed her greatly. In the dream, she saw her son's plane on fire and he was crying to her for help; then she saw the plane crash into the sea. She said that she knew her son was drowned.

Such was the torment from which she would awaken every morning for over a week, and her waking thoughts were charged with fear and foreboding.

I explained to this distraught mother, as best I could, that undoubtedly it was a premonition of disaster and that she, being tuned in subconsciously to her son, unquestionably had picked up his unconscious fear of danger. She could prevent it, though, as obviously it had not happened yet because she had received no official word; furthermore, the dream was recurring night after night, presaging that which was yet to come. I told her what to do, and that was to get her highest concept of God and His love.

She began to think of God as Infinite Life Principle of absolute love, boundless wisdom, all-powerful, all-bliss, all-peace, and absolute harmony and joy, and at my suggestion she mentally placed her son in God's loving care, realizing that her son is living in the secret place of the Most High and abiding under the shadow of the Almighty. She also pictured her son home—happy, joyous, and free—and she felt him embracing her.

This mother steered and directed her thoughts all day long to adhere to this spiritual pattern of prayer. She mentally dwelt on the light, love, power, and peace of God until it became real to her, and in that spiritual atmosphere she placed her son.

As she persevered along this line of thinking, the nightmare ceased to come after the fifth night. Her feeling toward her son had changed from fear to faith and confidence that he was whole and perfect and watched over by a benign Providence.

Some weeks later as she was preparing lunch, her son walked in the door and embraced her! He was home from Vietnam and wanted to surprise her. He said to her, "Mother, I don't know how I am alive! My plane crashed after being shot at, but it did not catch fire. I was unharmed, and the most extraordinary thing happened: I knew the plane was falling but I had no fear. I heard your voice clearly saying to me, 'God is watching over you,' and I knew I was safe."

The Bible says: *He shall give his angels charge over thee, to keep thee in all thy ways* (Ps. 91:11).

One thing is evident in this experience: the mother was telepathically *en rapport* with her son, as there is no time or space in mind, and through prayer she cleansed her mind of fear by enfolding her son with God's love, light, harmony, and peace. This opened the way for the response of a guiding Providence to free her son from a death that would otherwise have been inescapable.

Her faith and confidence were communicated to her son, and he experienced the joy of the answered prayer.

HOW A FATHER'S DREAM OF HIS SON'S DEATH HELPED AVERT THE TRAGEDY

This is what a correspondent from New York City said in his letter:

> Dear Dr. Murphy: How grateful I am is almost impossible to tell. I have been deeply impressed in reading *The Amazing Laws of Cosmic Mind Power*.[1] I have learned how to pray scientifically by studying each chapter. It has proved to be a revelation to me!
>
> One of my sons was doing long distance hauling between New York and Chicago. One night in a dream a few weeks ago, I saw his truck traveling up a hill and he seemed to be asleep. On the right side was a high mountain, and on the other side, a deep ravine. Suddenly the truck hit the cliff and fell over sideways. In my dream state, I said, "God watches over him. God cares for him, and God loves him."
>
> Then I woke up, my whole body shaking with apprehension of disaster. I opened the Bible and read aloud the 91st Psalm, the great Psalm of Protection, changing the tense to second person, and prayed for my boy for about one-half hour, starting off with *"He* dwells in the secret place . . . *He* abides under the shadow of the Almighty . . .," and so on. Gradually, a sense of peace came over me.
>
> Later during the week when my son came home, he told me that he had fallen asleep while driving the truck, which had turned over, and he had found himself under the truck between the wheels, miraculously saved and without a scratch. I then told him of my dream and of my prayer in the dream, and he said, "Dad, your prayer saved my life!"

HOW TO HELP PREVENT TRAGEDIES AND REVERSALS OF FORTUNE

Prayer does change things; countless biographies attest to that fact. By prayer, I mean the contemplation of the truths of God

---

[1] Joseph Murphy, *The Amazing Laws of Cosmic Mind Power* (West Nyack, N.Y.: Parker Publishing Company, Inc., 1965).

from the highest standpoint. By thinking constructively, based on universal principles, you may change all the negative patterns in your mind and thereafter bear a charmed life. In other words, by filling your mind with the truths of God, you would neutralize, obliterate, and expunge from your mind everything unlike God. You would avoid all negative experiences, such as accidents and disasters of all kinds. Your escape from ill fortune would coincide with your ability to rise in consciousness. *I, if I be lifted up . . . draw all men* (manifestations and experiences) *unto me* (John 12:32).

By contemplating the eternal verities and that which is true of God, you separate yourself from the mass mind, or the law of averages, which dominates the mass of humanity.

When you enter God's peace and let His peace flow through you like a golden river of life and love, you have touched Reality, or God, just as this father did while praying for his son.

"WHY IS IT THAT ONLY NEGATIVE PREDICTIONS REGARDING MY FUTURE COME TO PASS?"

The above question came to my desk from a correspondent in Alaska.

You must remember that your subconscious mind is a storehouse of memory and that many suggestions, half truths and false beliefs have been accepted, of which your conscious mind is wholly unaware. Many times these things come to pass, for whatever your subconscious mind is impregnated with becomes objectified in your world sooner or later, *unless changed by prayer* for the better.

In other words, any man receiving a suggestion or a prediction regarding himself, of an undesirable nature, can prevent it from coming to pass by thinking constructively upon the universal verities and truths of God, such as harmony, peace, love, beauty, Divine right action, and Divine love. In contemplating these universal principles, there takes place a *rearrangement of the patterns in his subconscious* to conform to the mental configuration of his thoughts and imagery.

It is possible to predict with a certain degree of accuracy for a person, a group, a race, a nation, or the world, because the majority of human beings do not change very much. They live with the same old beliefs, the same old traditions, race concepts, and the same hates, prejudices, and fears. They follow more or less a set pattern which can easily be read by those tuning in intuitively to their mental vibrations.

HOW PREVISION SOLVED A DOCTOR'S PROBLEM

A medical doctor friend was writing a book, and required special data about ancient medicine in Babylonia and Egypt. He thought that the information might be in a New York museum, but he was living in Los Angeles and it was impossible for him to go to New York.

I suggested to him that he still his mind, immobilize his attention, and just as he was about to go to sleep to speak authoritatively to his deeper mind as follows: "Infinite Intelligence within me knows the answer and It gives me the information I need for my book."

He dropped off to sleep with the one word, "answer," and the same night he had a dream which instructed him to visit an old book store downtown. On entering the book store, the first book he picked up gave him the desired data.

Remember that your subconscious is one with Infinite Intelligence and boundless wisdom, and is all-wise and knows what type of answer you desire. It may answer in a dream, as a hunch, or as a feeling that you are being led on the right track. You may get a sudden flash to go some place, or another person may give you the answer.

HOW CLAIRAUDIENCE SAVED A LIFE

Recently I spoke at a banquet, and a young officer who had recently returned from Vietnam sat next to me and told me a fascinating experience about the voice he heard from "nowhere."

He was under orders and was driving a jeep to deliver a message to his local headquarters. A junior officer sat beside him, and as they drove along the road at high speed, he heard his mother's voice say clearly and distinctly, "Stop! John. Stop! Stop!" He stopped the jeep suddenly, and his companion asked, "Why?

What's wrong?" and he said, "Didn't you hear the voice saying, 'Stop! Stop!'?" But his companion hadn't heard anything.

After getting out of the jeep and examining it they found one wheel loose; if they had gone another few yards, the car would have catapulted over a chasm on the side of the road and they would have been mangled beyond recognition.

His mother was in San Francisco, and he said that she prayed for him regularly every night and morning and also during the day, always claiming, "God's love and the whole armor of God surround my boy at all times."

This young man realized that the voice he had heard was a warning from his own subconscious mind, which sought to protect him and which undoubtedly had responded forcefully to his mother's prayer.

In times of great emergency or danger, you will find that your subconscious mind projects the voice of a person whom you will immediately obey, because you trust and love that person. It will speak to you only in a voice that your *conscious* mind will immediately accept as true. It would therefore not be the voice of someone whom you distrusted or disliked.

HOW TO PROTECT YOURSELF AND OTHERS FROM UNHAPPY EVENTS

You may have at times a precognitive dream accompanied by a deep intuitive feeling of impending danger for yourself or a loved one.

If your dream presages an unhappy or tragic occurrence relating to yourself or those close to you, do not deride it as a mere fabrication of your imagination or as a harmless hallucination.

Pray about the forewarning or presentiment as follows, and if your prayer is for someone else, use that person's name:

An effective protection prayer

"I realize that God is the only Presence and Power, and I know that God's Presence is love, order, beauty, peace, perfection, and harmony. God's inward peace flows through me now like a river. I recognize the perfect bliss and order which *is* and always has been.

I am immersed in the mind of God, and God sees me perfect, whole, and complete; I am immersed in the Holy Omnipresence. The whole armor of God surrounds me, enfolds me, and enwraps me, and underneath are the everlasting arms."

Affirm the truths in this prayer, and persevere until the cloud lifts and the burden is raised. You will enter into peace, and you will touch Reality. You will have consciously entered into union with the Higher Self, and then all the Divine forces will hasten to minister to your eternal joy.

What things soever ye desire, when ye pray, believe that ye receive them, and ye shall have them (Mark 11:24) .

POINTS TO RECALL IN THIS CHAPTER

1. One of the deeper faculties of your mind is your ability to have a prevision of things to come, sometimes as a dream and a vision in the depths of the night.
2. You can always ask for specific guidance from your subconscious mind about any venture, such as investments, trips, marriage, etc.
3. The future is already in your mind, because all the thoughts, beliefs, convictions, and impressions in your subconscious mind will, by the very law of your mind, become forms, functions, experiences, and events.
4. Dr. Rhine of Duke University in his experiments has documented experiments of clairvoyance, precognition, clairaudience, retrocognition, telekinesis, and other facets of extrasensory perception, commonly referred to as E.S.P.
5. A capable psychic or medium can communicate with or "tune in" on the contents of your subconscious and conscious mind, translating what she sees into her own terminology and predicting accordingly.
6. You may get different readings from different clairvoyants or mediums, as they filter what they see through their own mentalities, and for that reason they may vary somewhat with each medium.
7. The sense of intuition may become highly developed in you if you constantly claim that Infinite Intelligence is guiding you in all your ways.
8. If you have a relative in a war zone and have a vivid

dream of danger to him, pray for him by realizing that where he is, God is, and His love, light, truth, and power protect him and watch over him. With proper application you can prevent a tragedy.

9. You are always telepathically united with your loved ones, and your prayers for them can heal, bless, and protect them.

10. When you have a vivid, precognitive dream of danger for a son, daughter, or friend, read the great truths of the 91st Psalm, mentioning his or her name, until your mind enters into a state of rest in God.

11. Prayer changes the subconscious mind of yourself and the other person, thereby eliminating the cause of the impending tragedy or unhappy situation.

12. By contemplating the eternal verities, you come out of the mass mind or the law of averages, and you build up convictions counter to the mass mind, thereby establishing your immunity to danger.

13. Your subconscious mind is a storehouse of memory, and many suggestions, half truths, and false beliefs have been embedded in it. Fill your conscious mind with the truths of God, and you will eradicate and expunge from your subconscious all the negative patterns.

14. It is fairly easy to predict the future for the average person, as the majority of people do not change very much in their thought patterns.

15. It is possible for you to hear the distinct voice of your mother, even though you may be 10,000 miles away. Your subconscious selects a voice that you will instantly listen to and obey.

16. You can change any negative pattern seen in your mind by realizing the Presence and Power of God and by knowing that the Presence of God is the presence of order, harmony, peace, joy, wholeness, love, and perfection.

SIX

How Infinite Mind
Reveals Answers in Dreams
and the Meaning of
Out-of-Body Experiences

The Bible says: *In a dream, in a vision of the night, when deep sleep falleth upon men, in slumberings upon the bed; then he openeth the ears of men and sealeth their instruction* (Job 33:15, 16).

And being warned of God in a dream that they should not return to Herod, they departed into their own country another way (Matt. 2:12).

The Bible is replete with accounts of dreams, visions, revelations, and warnings occurring during sleep. When you are asleep, your subconscious mind is very much awake and continuously active, as it never sleeps. You will recall that Joseph correctly interpreted the dreams of Pharaoh and that they subsequently came to pass. His success in forecasting the future brought him prestige, honor and recognition by the king.

When you are dreaming, your conscious mind is suspended, and asleep. Your subconscious mind usually speaks in symbolic form, and this is why down through the ages men have employed dream expositors or interpreters. You are doubtless familiar with the fact that many Freudian and Jungian psychologists, psychiatrists and psychoanalysts and eclectic psychotherapeutists seriously study dreams, and try to interpret them to the conscious mind of the

54

patient. Often the explanations of the dreams lead to the uncovering of mental conflicts, phobias, fixations, and other mental complexes.

All your dreams are dramatizations of your subconscious and in many instances warn you of impending danger. Some dreams are definitely precognitive and can accurately probe the future. In other dreams you may get answers to your prayers. All dreams of a negative nature are subject to change and none is fatalistic.

Your subconscious, in its dream nature, is revealing to you the nature of the impressions made upon it and pointing out to you the course your life is taking. Research analyses of dreams show that the symbols appearing in the individual subconscious are personal and apply to each individual only; and the same symbol appearing in another dream can have still another and very different meaning.

In other words, your dream is personal and applies only to you, though it may show your relationship with another person.

AN INTERESTING DREAM ANALYZED

Some months ago, a student at the local university who had read my book, *The Power of Your Subconscious Mind*,[1] came in for an interview. During the course of the conversation, she said, "I have dreamt for three consecutive nights that I was present at a banquet for Governor Rockefeller of New York and that I sat next to him and was the guest of honor. What does it mean?" I explained to her that it was her dream and when interpreted it must be meaningful to her. I asked her what the significance of attending a banquet with Rockefeller meant to her. She immediately replied that it symbolizes wealth, prestige, honor and recognition. Then I added that it could well be that her subconscious was foreshadowing some special honor and recognition and, perhaps, also a shower of wealth. She seemed to agree with this and it seemed meaningful to her.

Two weeks later she won a scholarship enabling her to study in France, and her grandmother passed on bequeathing to her the sum of $50,000 for her education and personal use. In addition she

---

1 Joseph Murphy, *The Power of Your Subconscious Mind* (Englewood Cliffs, N.J.: Prentice-Hall, Inc., 1963) .

was invited to attend the inaugural banquet of Governor Reagan, which she did; and she had a wonderful time.

You will notice she did not take the dream in a literal sense. Your disciplined imaginative faculty, called "Joseph" in the Bible, can unclothe the dream of its form and see the hidden idea behind the symbol.

HOW A DREAM LED A WOMAN TO THE HOME SHE WANTED

A young married woman living in Beverly Hills experienced a recurrent dream for six consecutive nights. In her dream she walked all through the house she desired to buy, met the occupants, patted the dog and conversed with the Spanish maid in the latter's own language. She explored the garage, attic and all the rooms of the house.

On the following Sunday after church, she and her husband went for a ride. Passing the Brentwood area, she saw the house she had dreamed about with a sign "For sale by owner, Open house." Both of them went in; the owner of the house, his wife, the maid, and the dog all seemed unusually frightened and startled. The dog began to growl and its hair stood on end.

After a few minutes, the owner apologized and said, "We have seen a woman like you walk up and down our stairs several times at night and early in the morning. Our maid was frightened out of her wits and the dog growled and barked wildly as if he saw something weird."

The explanation is simple for this dream

This young woman explained to them that she had been praying for the right home and that every night she asked the Infinite Intelligence of her subconscious mind to direct her to the ideal home which would be spacious, lovely, central and ideal in every way.

Undoubtedly, as she went to sleep with the idea of a home uppermost in her mind, she charged her subconscious with a mission which *it had to fulfill*. Suddenly, while dreaming, she found herself outside her physical body but possessing a rarefied and attenuated sense of her own being which enabled her to travel through closed doors and to "collapse" time and space. She found herself in this house and became acquainted with all the parts of it, as well as with the occupants. She told them that she, too, was startled when she met them, as she had seen them several times before in the dream state.

Her "real" extrasensory travel

This woman projected her astral body and was perceived as an apparition by the people in the home where she visited. This perception was visual and auditory, as they heard her footsteps and saw her clearly. This young woman perceived her own physical body on the bed in her home and knew that she was traveling and operating in her fourth dimensional body. Such projected bodies may be perceived as ghosts or apparitions by people who are very sensitive and are psychically attuned to higher vibrations or a psychic demonstration.

This young woman and her husband purchased the home, and there was a very harmonious atmosphere throughout the proceedings for the transfer of title to the home.

HOW THE AUTHOR'S DREAM BECAME A LIVING EXPERIENCE

I once visited Yoga Forest University, at Rishikesh, India, north of New Delhi, for the purpose of lecturing there. Several nights before I enplaned for the trip I had experienced vivid dreams of the place, and I met all the teachers and students in my dreams.

Upon my arrival I discovered I knew my way around the premises. All the houses, lecture halls, teachers and students were very familiar to me. I pointed out to one of the attendants the room set aside for me, and I described its appearance inside, as well as the kind of food he was going to serve me. I even told him what he was going to say next, as I had heard his voice before. He was amazed and said, "You must be clairvoyant and clairaudient."

I explained the experience this way to him. Knowing that I was
going to lecture at Yoga Forest University and while sound asleep,
my subtle body, sometimes referred to as the astral body (which
has exactly the same shape as my physical body but is oscillating
and vibrating at a much higher frequency, but nevertheless is a
"body") traveled there, making my vivid dream a subsequent
conscious experience.

In other words, I went there in my astral body, conversed
mentally, but naturally, with many people, and heard their re-
sponses and voices. Furthermore, in that marvelous psychic kind of
astral journey, I viewed all the beauties of the Ganges River, the
Himalaya Mountains, and the loveliness of the countryside.

"I saw you before in a dream"

When I introduced myself to Yogi Sivenanda, who was directing
the Ashram, he exclaimed, "I saw you before several times in my
dreams, and I also heard your voice!" I explained to him that the
experience was mutual; that I had been visualizing a wonderful
trip and had impressed my subconscious mind and "went to sleep
on it." I further explained that I had also met him subjectively in
a dream state which became actualized, because while my body was
asleep in Beverly Hills, California, I found myself in a new body
visiting all the places in his Ashram and hearing all the voices.
Now, when I consciously and objectively arrived, I concretely
experienced all the states subjectively felt during my extrasensory
travel. In other words, what I saw and heard objectively, I had
previously seen and heard subjectively.

In his dreams, Yogi Sivenanda clairvoyantly saw me, and being
clairaudient, he heard my voice, as you can think, speak, act, travel
and even move all kinds of objects outside your body. You can see
and be seen, you can understand and be understood, and you can
also communicate messages and report on everything you see. All
your faculties, such as sight, hearing, taste, smell and touch, can be
duplicated in mind alone independent of your five senses. This
proves conclusively that you can live outside your present body
and that the Creative Intelligence within you intended that you
should use these faculties transcending your present environment's
three-dimensional body.

HOW HIS DREAM TRIED TO PROTECT HIS HEALTH

A man apparently in perfect health dreamed on several occasions that he was being operated on for a disorder of the prostate gland. He asked me if I thought he should see a doctor for a checkup but stated that he had no symptoms or pain of any kind. He had come to see me regarding a marital problem of an emotional nature. I clarified the workings of his subconscious mind to some degree; namely, that it seeks to protect him at all costs and that, undoubtedly, *the subconscious was prompting him regarding the imminence of some organic lesion or malfunctioning*. The subconscious reasons deductively from a basis of reality and thus revealed it to him in the form of a dream. He understood that his dream was personal and that any explanation or interpretation must agree with his intuitive perception.

I suggested that he should see his physician immediately and get a complete checkup by a urologist. However, he deferred seeing his doctor. In a few days' time he developed a urinary constriction and blockage and was in excruciating pain. His physician took him to the hospital and had a skilled urologist operate on him immediately. I visited him in the hospital shortly after that and he remarked to me, "I should have paid more attention to my dream and acted sooner." However, I am happy to say he made a wonderful recovery, as he continued to fill his subconscious mind with thoughts of wholeness, harmony, vitality and perfect health.

You will perceive that his subconscious mind was actually warning him to do something, as it knew of the prostatic infection and enlargement. The foreshadowing idea, the presentiment that he was going to be operated on, was probably caused by the already existing condition. He had made an error though in delaying a medical examination.

The words of the ancient proverb are true—"Night (sleep) brings counsel." The key to its practical application can be developed through your psychic awareness.

THE DIFFERENT TYPES OF DREAMS

There are several kinds of dreams, many of which are due to stomach disorders, mental and emotional turmoil, bodily discomfort, repressed or abnormal sex urges, and various fears and super-stitious beliefs.

However, there are also dreams wherein you see a future event before it happens, dreams which give you a definite answer to your prayer, and often you are given instruction as to taking action in the dream state.

HOW A DREAM WARNED A WOMAN ENGAGED
TO BE MARRIED

A young lady told me of a remarkable answer she received in a dream. At night as she went to sleep, she affirmed, "Infinite Intel-ligence in my subconscious mind reveals to me the answer regard-ing my proposed marriage to ————." During the night she had a rather strange dream in which she saw her fiancé in prison garb behind bars and a guard outside his cell with a gun. A man ap-peared in the dream and said, "Don't you recognize this man?"

She awakened suddenly quite perturbed and intuitively, through her dream, perceived that the man in her dream was her betrothed. She phoned her brother, who was a detective in the local police force, and he checked up on her fiancé. Her brother discovered that this man had a wife in New York City whom he had deserted, and furthermore that he had spent five years of his life in prison, all of which he had concealed from her. She broke off her engagement immediately and was deeply grateful for that inner guide which always seeks to protect you if you will only listen.

I, the Lord, will make myself known unto him in a vision, and will speak to him in a dream (Num. 12:6) .

HOW TO PREPARE YOUR MIND PRIOR TO SLEEP

When you enter into a drowsy, sleepy state, there is an outcrop-ping of your subconscious mind and you are in a highly sensitized mental condition. The thought and feeling you have prior to sleep is immediately transmitted to your subconscious mind, which then begins to act on your request or desire for guidance. The creative power of your subconscious mind is waiting to respond and act upon whatever desires, ideas and instructions you consciously issue in your "awake" state of mind.

Remember also that your subconscious mind is impersonal and nonselective—it will accept your negative, resentful or hateful thoughts, as well as the good thoughts, and act accordingly. The subconscious magnifies and multiplies whatever you deposit in it, *good or bad;* hence, it is extremely important for you to cleanse your mind of all disturbing, vexatious thoughts of any kind, thus creating a clear channel for the Divine energies to flow through you constructively.

An effective technique
to follow every night

Look over the events of the day; and whatever strife, contentions or vexations may have occurred, affirm to yourself quietly, "I fully and freely forgive myself for harboring these negative thoughts and for the negative way I handled and responded to this or that problem. I resolve to handle these problems in the right way the next time. I radiate love, peace, joy and goodwill to all those around me and to all people everywhere. God's love fills my soul and I rejoice in the success and happiness of my associates and all men and women everywhere. I am at peace. I sleep in peace tonight, I wake in joy, and I live in God. I give thanks for the joy of the answered prayer."

HOW A MOTHER'S DREAM PROTECTED
HER DAUGHTER

Recently I received a letter from a woman, who said that she had been using the prayers suggested in one of my books, *Miracle of Mind Dynamics,*[2] for herself and her daughter. She had a harrowing dream one night wherein she saw her high school age daughter raped and strangled by a young boy. The dream took place in an automobile on a country road. The whole experience was a frightening nightmare, and she woke up screaming.

She decided to act on the forewarning, *knowing there was no*

---

[2] Joseph Murphy, *Miracle of Mind Dynamics* (Englewood Cliffs, N.J.: Prentice-Hall, Inc., 1964).

such thing as inexorable fate and that the tragedy could be pre-vented by tuning in on God and praying. She prayed as follows: "My daughter is a child of God. Where she is God is. God is all harmony, peace, beauty, love, joy and power. My daughter is immersed in the Holy Presence of God and the whole armor of God surrounds her. She is watched over by God, her Loving Father. She dwells in the secret place of the most High and abides in the shadow of the Almighty." After meditating about ten minutes, the mother felt a sense of peace and tranquility and went back to sleep.

In the morning she called her daughter by long distance but could not reach her at the school, because it was a holiday in that state. During the day she continued praying for her daughter. At night her daughter called her and said, "Mother, you appeared to me last night in my dream and begged me not to go out riding with one of the boys in the school because he was very aggressive and I would certainly regret it. I felt terribly upset. In the morning, I had a phone call from him asking me to go for a ride with him out in the country. I refused, pleading illness.

"My girl friend went with him, against my pleadings, because I told her my dream. He raped her and almost choked her to death. She is now in the hospital and the police are hunting the boy, who disappeared from his house."

There is a telepathic communication at all times between members of the family and loved ones or close friends. The mother's prayer for her daughter was received subjectively by the daughter, which prevented a potential disaster in her life.

The Bible says, *For He will give His angels charge over thee, to keep thee in all thy ways. They shall bear thee up in their hands, lest thou dash thy foot against a stone* (Ps. 91:11, 12).

POINTS TO RECALL IN THIS CHAPTER

1. Dreams are dramatizations of your subconscious mind, usually appearing in symbolic form. Your disciplined imagination can unclothe the dream and reveal its hidden content.
2. Some dreams are precognitive, whereby you see a future event before it happens. The reason for this is that in the mind principle there is no time or space.

3. Dreams of a negative nature may be counteracted by tuning in on the God Presence within you and identifying mentally and emotionally with the truths of God, thereby transforming the negative patterns in your subconscious mind.

4. It is possible through astral travel to be guided to the right home, to visit that home and see the occupants and all the furnishings.

5. When asleep and in a deep dream state, it may be possible to project your psychic body, which can be perceived as an apparition or vision by others.

6. Some years ago, I had a deep and vivid dream. I found myself outside my body thousands of miles away in Yoga Forest University, India, where I entered all the buildings and saw the teachers and students by means of extrasensory travel.

7. You can see, hear, feel, smell, taste and travel independently of your physical organism. All the faculties of your senses can be duplicated in your mind. Therefore, it was intended you use these faculties and powers independently of your physical body and environment.

8. You may dream of being operated on. This may be the the intuitive voice of your subconscious warning you of some present lesion in your body or some malfunction of one of your organs. It may be wise to get a medical checkup. The intimations and urges of your subconscious are lifeward.

9. There are all kinds of dreams. If you go to sleep angry and resentful, your subconscious mind may dramatize these negative impressions as nightmares, such as a tiger attacking you, etc. Go to sleep every night in the spirit of forgiveness and goodwill to all.

10. A good technique to practice prior to sleep is to cleanse your mind of all negatives and to fill your mind with the truths of God, wishing love and goodwill to all. Affirm, "I sleep in peace, I wake in joy, and I live in God."

11. The Bible says, *"I, the Lord, will make myself known unto him in a vision and will speak unto him in a dream"* (Num. 12:6). This is your Divine authority.

SEVEN

How Infinite Mind Solves Problems and Saves Lives Through the Mystery of Dream Impressions

I have found in my counseling experience that people of all walks of life are fascinated by dreams. Today in medical research laboratories, teams of psychologists and doctors are conducting experiments on the dream life of men and women, and they have come to the conclusion that all people dream; furthermore, in extensive test cases, these scientists have discovered that when the subjects are awakened periodically while dreaming, this deprivation of dream life may bring on mental, emotional, and even physical disturbances.

Many people are familiar with the names of Freud, Jung, and Adler, who have acquired fame for having delved into the dream life of their patients. Through their studies of the dreams of their subjects, these men have evolved different schools of psychology, namely Psychoanalysis (Freud), Analytical Psychology (Jung), and Individual Psychology (Adler). All three have written extensively in the field of dreams, and their interpretations and conclusions vary considerably. These differences are so conflicting and at variance that I shall not even begin to discuss them here.

The purpose of this chapter and this book, however, is to show that the key to solving your problem often comes as a clear-cut and definite answer in a dream.

HOW BILLY SOLVED HIS PROBLEM
THROUGH A DREAM

Billy is twelve years old. He hears my lectures occasionally, as I suggest to parents that all boys and girls twelve years of age and older should attend; they are quite able to understand this teaching.

Billy told me that his mother gave him a book to read, *Treasure Island*, which is about Hawaii. He read it avidly, and knowing to some degree how his subconscious mind works, every night prior to sleep he spoke to his subconscious mind (which he calls "Subby") as follows: "Subby, I am going to Hawaii for my vacation. I am going by plane, and I'll swim in the ocean, ride a bicycle over one of the islands, and live in a penthouse. I want a clear answer, please."

He did not discuss this with his brother, father, or mother. Following these suggestions to his subconscious mind, he had a dream wherein he clearly saw a penthouse, the name of a hotel—Maui Hilton—and the Island of Maui in the chain of the Hawaiian Islands. He said to his mother the next day, "Mom, we are going to Hawaii for our vacation," and he gave her all the details.

She laughed and said, "Well, this is news to me! Where did you get that idea?"

Billy replied, "All I know is that we are going, and we'll live in a penthouse at a hotel." His mother dismissed the dream as one of the vagaries of a young mind.

Two weeks later, Billy's father (who knew nothing about the dream), because of his son's excellent grades in school, suggested that Bill's mother go with both the boys on a vacation to Hawaii, which he had come to know and love during his stay there as a Naval officer; he said he would pay all the expenses involved.

Billy yelled, "I told you, Mom! We're going to Hawaii!" Every detail of this boy's dream was fulfilled, including the penthouse, exactly as he saw it.

You will notice that this dream was experienced clearly by the boy. The subconscious mind is amenable to suggestion, and you will also note that Billy said, "I want a clear answer"; his subconscious mind responded accordingly.

THE IMPORTANCE OF DREAMING LITERALLY

For several years I have been suggesting to my subconscious prior to sleep, "I dream literally and clearly, and I remember my dream." It seems that over a period of time I have convinced my subconscious mind, inasmuch as close to 90 per cent of my dreams are literal in the same way you read your morning newspaper. I receive many answers to my prayers in dreams.

Your conscious mind can and does direct the activities of your mind in sleep. You can stop the recurrence of "bad dreams," nightmares, or dreams that you dread. Your conscious mind[1] controls your subconscious, and you can alter the nature of your dreams by using your capacity to choose and reject thoughts and ideas that you use in disciplining your reflections and fancies during the day. In this way, the habit of dream-control gradually will come under your own jurisdiction.

How my dream saved a life

A member of my congregation called me on the phone and asked me to give her a blessing on her approaching journey to Europe, which I did, affirming something like this: "Divine love and harmony go before you, making joyous, happy, and glorious your way. God's messengers of life, love, truth, and beauty watch over you at all times, and whatever means of conveyance you use represents God's idea moving from point to point freely, joyously, and lovingly. You are always in the secret vault of the Most High, and you are watched over by the Overshadowing Presence."

That night I had a dream in which I clearly saw this woman in England purchasing a ticket for France, and I saw the plane she would be on going down in flames. I phoned her the next morning and told her that I usually dream literally, due to suggestions to my subconscious mind. I asked her if she planned a trip to France while in Europe, and she said, "Yes." Then I told her what I had seen in my dream and advised her not to go on the plane to France.

---

[1] Joseph Murphy, *The Power of Your Subconscious Mind* (Englewood Cliffs, N.J.: Prentice-Hall, Inc., 1963).

She replied, "I'm so grateful you called! My brother in the next dimension appeared to me last night in my dream and said, 'Sis, don't dare go on that plane in England scheduled for Perpignan, France'; then he disappeared. I have already cancelled my trip, as I have an overwhelming inner feeling that it would be disastrous."

Subsequently, headlines in the news revealed the fatal trip in which 88 people were killed.

Having read this far in the book, you will readily see the cause of the dreams. As we prayed together over the phone, we impregnated and activated our subconscious mind, which sees all and knows all, and it responded symbolically in her case and literally in my case.

Self-preservation is the first law of life, and your subconscious always seeks to protect and to preserve you from harm of every kind. Remember, also, that harmony and discord do not dwell together; therefore, she could not be on an airplane that caught fire, as she had claimed that Divine love and harmony go before her, making straight and joyous her way.

The appearance of her brother was a dramatization of her subconscious mind; it is All-Wise and knows the voice you will listen to. Her brother had brought her up, as their father had died when she was very young; he had played the role of father to his sister, had sent her to college, and had paid all her expenses. He had passed on to the next dimension some months prior to her dream.

HOW A BOY CONTROLLED HIS SUBCONSCIOUS IN A DREAM

A young boy who had been reading and listening to ghost stories was brought to me by his mother. Night after night, a ghost-like man, dressed in a white sheet and having a frightful looking face, said to the boy, "I'm taking you away. You're a bad boy." This dream was devastating to the child, for he would wake up screaming and crying every night.

I suggested to the boy that he cease reading ghost stories, because his deeper mind magnified the thoughts and pictures held by his conscious mind prior to sleep. I also suggested, "When the ghostly old man comes in your dream, be friendly to him, as he is probably a lonesome old man and really loves boys; he wants you to be friendly with him. Maybe he lost a son and is trying to be friendly with a boy who resembles his son. Tonight when you go to sleep, if he comes to you, say, 'Hi, there; I'm your friend and I love you.' Shake his hand and offer to give him a few cookies your mother makes."

That night he took the cookies to bed with him and put them under his pillow, and when the man appeared, his mother, who was sleeping in the next bed to him, heard him say in his sleep, "Hi, there. I'm your friend and I love you. Here are some cookies for you. My mother makes them, and they are good," and the boy fetched the cookies from under the pillow and offered them to the ghostly figure. Then his overwhelming fear abated. He became relaxed and fell into a deep, restful, and natural sleep, and he became free from his horrible nightmare.

He had accepted the suggestions I gave him and he followed the directions, which counteracted the fearsome impressions with which he had unconsciously impregnated his mind. He made friends in his sleep with the so-called specter, and he brought peace to his troubled mind.

HOW YOU CAN CHANGE A DISTURBING DREAM

Many people who read murder and detective stories or watch violent dramas on television take these disturbing thoughts and pictures into their subconscious mind as they retire in sleep. Their deeper mind magnifies and dramatizes exceedingly everything impressed upon it, and these people suffer and experience nightmares where lions, tigers and other wild animals attack them. I have instructed many troubled people to affirm prior to sleep: "I know why I am dreaming this way, and I know it is a dream. I remain dreaming, and the nightmare ceases and is switched off. God's love fills my soul, and I dream in peace all night and I wake in joy."

Invariably this technique works. Anyone may carry out this simple method in curing nightmares resulting from reading ghost stories, murder stories, or from watching warlike movies or television programs of a psychopathic nature.

My suggestion to everybody is to read several times prior to sleep one of the beautiful Psalms, such as the 23rd, 27th, 42nd, 46th, 91st, or 100th. Then you will neutralize any noxious patterns in your subconscious and impress it instead with whatever things are lovely and of good report. What you impress on the subconscious is always expressed as form, function, experience, and event.

HOW A COURT JUDGE GOT AN ANSWER IN A DREAM

A local court judge, who is a member of my club, told me of a most interesting dream. For about five consecutive nights he had dreamt that he was looking at a street sign which read "Murphy Street," and then he was with a crowd of people at the Wilshire Ebell Theatre at Wilshire and Lucerne Boulevards in Los Angeles, where I give public lectures. He did not see me in the dream, but the dream troubled him; he spoke to his wife about it, and she suggested that he talk to me about it.

I replied, "Generally speaking, when a certain dream occurs repeatedly night after night, your subconscious is redramatizing it because it is very important to you, in the same way that in your judicial process, you may lay stress on a vital point of law which is essential for the jury to know." I added that his dream was personal and that any explanation must coincide with his own viewpoint.

I said that my own intuitive perception of the dream was that while no "Murphy Street" exists near the Wilshire Ebell Theatre, his subconscious mind for its own reasons wanted him to take in the following Sunday's lecture on "The Spiritual Approach to Injustice"; the symbolic meaning of "Murphy Street" undoubtedly was referring to the speaker (myself) .

The judge seemed to be deep in thought, and then he said, "That's right. I have spent some sleepless nights over a decision I am to make, and I have wondered about the spiritual approach to all these things, for there are so many inequities and injustices all over the world since man appeared."

He came to the lecture that Sunday, and on shaking hands with me as he left, he said, "You were right and my dream was right. I got the answer, and I know what my decision will be now."

The ways of your subconscious are beyond discovery. The Bible, in referring to the workings of your subconscious mind, delineates it in these words: *For my thoughts are not your thoughts, neither are your ways my ways, saith the Lord. For as the heavens are higher than the earth, so are my ways higher than your ways, and my thoughts than your thoughts* (Isa. 55:8–9).

AN ANSWER TO A BIBLE STUDENT'S DREAM

Recently I had a visit from a college student who is in his fourth year of studies in a seminary, and he remarked that Freud's pioneer definition was that a dream symbolizes a wish fulfilled, but that it certainly did not fit his particular dream.

In our discussion, I said that his subconscious mind could project in dream form anything which may be seriously troubling him; that when the everyday, surface mind, deeply preoccupied with Biblical or religious studies, thinks of any person, this may very well find symbolic expression in Biblical verses or person-alities in dream form; and that all he had to do was to read the vision of Peter in Acts 10, beginning with verse 9, and see how the dilemma of Peter was completely solved in a dream when the voice of intuition spoke to him, saying: . . . *What God hath cleansed, that call not thou common* (Acts 10:15).

The Bible student's dream

For several nights while in deep sleep, this Bible student saw a shining sword and a man, who seemed to be Jesus, waving the sword; then he saw the words "I come not to bring peace but a sword."

He said to me, "What does it mean? I asked my professor, and he said, 'Oh, forget it. It's only a dream. You have been reading the Bible, and in phantasy you saw what you were reading.' "

The young man said, "I am terribly disturbed. I have been going to a psychiatrist attached to our religious institution. He gave me tranquilizers, and they have quieted me. But I am seri-ously questioning everything I read and hear and am being taught. I can't take the Bible literally; I believe all men are sons of God, that God is no respecter of persons, and that no creed or church has a monopoly on truth."

My interpretation
and his reaction

The Biblical accounts of dream interpretation indicate the importance of prophetic and Divinely inspired dreams, which are so numerous in both the Old and the New Testaments. The Bible language is symbolic, figurative, and allegorical, and all the stories of the Bible arose from the subconscious minds of inspired writers.

The sword is an age-old symbol of Truth, of the God-Presence within man which severs him from superstition, ignorance, false beliefs, and fears of all kinds. When man learns the truth of his being and the workings of his conscious and subconscious mind, he learns that he is the master of his own destiny. The Truth stirs up man, creates a quarrel in his mind, and challenges all his false indoctrination, creeds, dogmas, and traditions, and speaks to him of a God of love.

The sword of Truth separates the chaff from the wheat, the false from the real. It represents Divine reasoning, whereby you judge from the standpoint of universal truths and not from the standpoint of man-made theology, the opinions of men, liturgies, and ceremonies.

I explained to this young man, "Your dream is telling you to reason things out for yourself, not upon appearances or theological complexities, but upon reason based on mental and spiritual laws which are just as valid as are the laws of chemistry, physics, or mathematics.

"The God-Presence in you is telling you to sever yourself completely from your present beliefs and to accept the Divinity within you, which responds to all men. Come to a decision based upon the cosmic, universal truths of God, the same yesterday, today, and forever. The Divine Truth in you will not let you rest until you believe in the goodness of God, the love of God, the harmony of God, and the joy of the Lord, which is your strength."

There was a terrible conflict in this young man's mind: he was professing to believe with his lips that which his heart felt to be false. This conflict had brought about almost a complete mental breakdown, resulting in the need for psychiatric attention and medication. But when the effects of the drugs wore off, the mental infection, or trauma, reared its ugly head again and said, "Here I am. Solve me!" And the dream reappeared.

The solution

He remarked, "Every word that you said feels true in my heart. Regardless of my parents and what they think, I'm quitting immediately and will practice what I really believe."

He is now studying psychology in the university and the science of the mind and *The Power of Your Subconscious Mind.*[2] He has married a lovely girl and is extremely happy in his new studies. He has decided to become a non-denominational minister and to give to people the psychological and spiritual interpretation of the Scriptures.

HOW THE BIBLE ANSWERED THE PRAYER OF A PRIEST

Some time ago, I had dinner with a relative of mine who is a priest in a very prominent parish. He had been having much difficulty with a few leading members of his church and also with his bishop, and he had been praying for guidance from God about how to solve his problem.

"Joe," he said, "you teach the inner meaning of the Bible, which I don't go along with altogether, but I agree with some of your teaching. What do you make of this dream which I have had four or five times in the last few months? I have seen these words from Proverbs in my dream: *Turn not to the right hand nor to the left: remove thy foot from evil* (Prov. 4:27).

"Well, Tom," I said, "I'm sure you know the meaning of that as well as I do, and it most certainly is an answer to your prayer for Divine guidance. All it means is that you don't do anything at all about the situation either objectively [right hand] or subjectively [left hand], i.e., there's nothing more to pray about.

"*Foot,* in Biblical symbology, means understanding, and *to remove your foot from evil* means to stop worrying and thinking

---

[2] Joseph Murphy, *The Power of Your Subconscious Mind* (Englewood Cliffs, N.J.: Prentice-Hall, Inc., 1963).

negatively about it, as your *evil* would be to give power to others or to conditions and not to give all power to God within you."

He said, "You mean I should sit still, say nothing and do nothing more, and let God work it out?"

"Yes," I said, "that's exactly what I mean. But if it does not mean the same thing to you, obviously it is not the right interpretation."

Tom said, "Yes, it is. I know!"

In about a month's time, the bishop, who had been critical of him, passed away, and the men who were creating trouble and wanted to oust him were transferred by their respective organizations to other cities.

A few nights ago, Tom called me long distance and said, "Joe, that dream was right. Why did it come in a dream?"

My reply was, "All I know, Tom, is that the Bible says . . . *I will speak unto him in a dream* (Num. 12:6) ."

POINTS TO RECALL IN THIS CHAPTER

1. People have always been interested in dreams. All people dream, and so do animals. Tensions are released in dreams, and many answers to our prayers come in dreams.

2. Interpretation of dreams and their importance have varied in the different psychological schools. Often, however, the answer to a perplexing problem comes to you in a dream as a clear-cut answer to your prayer.

3. A little boy suggested to his subconscious what he wished to come to pass and the way he wanted it; then he suggested that the answer be given to him clearly so that he could understand it. The subconscious mind, amenable to suggestion, responded accordingly.

4. As a rule, your subconscious speaks to you symbolically in dreams; however, you can suggest to your subconscious every night, "I dream literally and clearly," and since it is the seat of habit, your constant reiteration of that suggestion prior to sleep causes your subconscious to speak to you in literal terms.

5. Our minds are one, and in the mind principle there is no time or space. It is therefore possible for you to see the

answer in a dream for another person for whom you have
been praying.

6. A judge, wondering what decision to make in a special
   case, received an answer to his request by understanding
   symbolism in his dreams.

7. Anyone suffering nightmares which may be due to ghost
   stories or murder stories, or seeing wild west movies and
   the like on television, can change his nightmares by constructive suggestions to the subconscious mind prior to
   sleep.

8. Bible students may get answers to their dreams in prayer
   requests by certain verses from the Bible or by the symbolic appearance of a Biblical personality, quoting a certain paragraph of the Bible, which reveals the answer.

9. A priest, wondering what decision to make, has a recurrent dream wherein he sees a quotation from the Book of
   Proverbs instructing him not to turn to the right or the
   left, in other words, to stand still and do nothing. He followed the Biblical injunction as seen in his dream, and it
   was a perfect answer to his prayer.

10. The ways of your subconscious are beyond explanation,
    and the Bible, in speaking of your subconscious, says:
    . . . *I will speak unto him in a dream* (Num. 12:6) .

EIGHT

How to Tune In with the Infinite and How to Make Extrasensory Perception Work for You

This book deals with the mental key for the solution of human problems. I have discovered that the answers to the most perplexing problems which beset man come from within the realm of the subconscious mind. When a boy of about nine years of age, I became deeply interested in the higher function of the mind and marveled at what we now call the intuitive and psychic powers that solve the problems of farmers living in remote sections of the countryside.

HOW EXTRASENSORY PERCEPTION HELPED FIND A MISSING SON

A farmer whom we shall call Jerry lived a quarter of a mile from me, and when I was very young, I used to visit him in the fields and found a distinct joy in helping him in various ways. One day he discovered his boy was missing. Night came and the boy had not returned. Jerry was distraught and grief stricken. He called the neighbors, and a group of men set out on horseback to look for him, for acquaintances had heard the boy say that he was going to climb Mount Kidd, a mountain in a remote area of West Cork, Ireland, near our home. The searchers, however, could find no trace of the boy. Night came and they had to end their search.

During his sleep that night, my distraught neighbor, Jerry, had a vivid dream. He perceived through extrasensory perception where his boy was. The location was familiar to him, and he saw the boy asleep near a certain rock with bushes over him. Therefore, at daybreak he got on his donkey and headed for the spot in the mountain he had viewed in his dream. He tied his donkey and climbing by foot to the exact spot, he found his son sleeping under the bushes. With great relief and happiness he awakened the boy, and though his son was surprised to see his father, he said to him, "I prayed that you would find me."

This farmer had revealed, as countless thousands of others have, the power of extrasensory perception to solve their problems. I might add that this farmer never went to school and did not know how to read or write. He certainly knew nothing whatever about the laws of the mind or ESP. The words "telepathy," "clairvoyance" and "precognition" would have been meaningless to him.

I remember asking Jerry, "How did you know where Jeremiah (his son) was?" He answered, "God told me in a dream."

The answer, as I see it, was rather simple. He was thinking of his son and wondering where he was before he fell asleep, and he probably prayed in his simple way to God. His subconscious mind then revealed the answer to him in a clairvoyant vision.

HOW YOU CAN USE EXTRASENSORY PERCEPTION

I have talked with hundreds of people who have informed me of getting specific data and information which they could not have received through the normal five sense channels. In every case they had concentrated on answers and their deeper mind responded as dreams and visions of the night, and in intuitive flashes.

How a woman became aware of her extrasensory perception

Some years ago, let us call her Mrs. Jean Wright, accompanied by her husband and guests, visited the race track at Agua Caliente. At that time she was not the slightest bit interested in paranormal or psychic experiences, or in the workings of her deeper or inner mind. That night prior to sleeping, she was contemplating the races the following day and wondering what to wear. She began to think about the fact that she had never attended a race track in her life and knew nothing about the horses, jockeys or even how to bet on a race. Prior to sleep, she said to herself, "I hope I will know what to do and that I will have a couple of winners, as all I am going to bet is four dollars—two dollars in each of two races.

She is very intuitive and quite psychic, and she dreams of many future events. That night she envisioned two horses named Robby's Choice and Billy's Friend as winners. Intuitively she felt they were going to win. (The names of her two sons are Robby and Billy.)

When they arrived at the race track the next morning, she inquired of her husband how to bet and he showed her. She placed her money on the two horses named Robby's Choice and Billy's Friend, and both came in over twenty to one.

Her subconscious mind, which is the source of all extrasensory perception, responded to her concentrated thought prior to sleep. Her focused attention was on two winners, which impregnated her subconscious mind. The latter responded accordingly, giving her two winners, for which she asked casually and without undue mental stress or strain.

EXTRASENSORY PERCEPTION IN ACTION

One of the foremost research investigations in the study of extrasensory phenomena has been conducted by Professor J. B. Rhine of Duke University. Professor Rhine has published several books on the subject and has lectured on the topic in many countries and before scientific bodies. He has gathered an enormous amount of material—well authenticated and documented—on the extraordinary power of the mind. He is especially interested in clairvoyance—the awareness, without the use of your normal senses, of what is going on elsewhere in the world, thus enabling you to see such events clearly.

He has also elaborated at length on precognition (seeing future events before they happen); telepathy (the transference of thought from one mind to another); telekinesis (the action of your mind on external objects or matter without any physical contacts); and retrocognition (your ability to see the past). It is interesting to read about academic laboratories, here and in Europe and India, that use the modus operandi of laboratory equipment; and of scientific studies over many years that set forth that these extrasensory perception faculties are in all of us, but that they also follow certain basic laws of mental action.

Her extrasensory perception
enabled her to see
a funeral procession

My youngest sister Elizabeth, when she was about five years of age, shouted out loud in the yard outside our home where all five of us were playing (two brothers and three sisters) that she saw a funeral procession; that Grandmother was dead. She named the priest who was leading the procession and saw that our father and mother were following in a horse and carriage. All of us laughed at her, and Mother rebuked her for being so naughty and evil as to say Grandmother was dead when we all knew very well that she was very much alive. Grandmother lived about fifteen miles away. At that time there was no such thing as phone service or telegraphic communication in that remote part of the country. Communication was by messenger on foot, horseback or donkey.

That same evening a relative hurried to our home announcing Grandmother's death and asking my father and mother to attend the wake and funeral. The messenger said that she died at 2:00 P.M., which was about the time my sister, Elizabeth, saw the funeral and the priest leading the procession.

This faculty of extrasensory perception is called precognition, since the funeral procession (as Elizabeth had described) took place the following day and the priest she named conducted the funeral service. Unfortunately, due to criticism and ridicule of her intuitive faculties, as time passed her quality of extrasensory perception was inhibited and suppressed. Gradually, her precognitive faculty more or less atrophied.

An outstanding case of
traveling clairvoyance

The classic case is that of the famous Emanuel Swedenborg, authenticated and scrutinized by the equally famous Immanuel

Kant. Swedenborg, while talking to a group of scientists at Gö-teborg, Sweden, had a clairvoyant vision, wherein he perceived clearly the origin and course of a great fire at Stockholm over 250 miles away. He also described in detail the extinction of the fire. A few days later, messengers from Stockholm arrived and attested to the accuracy of his clairvoyant vision.

This demonstrates that within each one of us there are tran-scendental powers which can project themselves beyond the limi-tations of time and space.

EXTRASENSORY PERCEPTION IS ACTIVE EVERYWHERE

On a recent trip to San Francisco, a woman sat next to me on the airplane. She seemed terribly upset and distraught. She offered me a paper to read. Suddenly I had an overpowering urge to ask her, "Have you left your husband?" So, I did just that! She seemed to be taken aback and said, "Yes. Why do you ask?" "Because I intuitively sense it," I answered.

She said, "Oh! You are one of those psychic people who see things." I said, "No—not that, but occasionally I get subliminal uprushes from my subconscious mind which reveal answers to me. I believe this comes to anyone who practices the laws of the mind and the way of the Infinite Spirit within man."

"Oh, I see," she said. "I left my husband this morning and I am going off to Australia with a man in San Francisco as soon as his divorce is final. Now I don't know whether I'm doing the right thing or not. I'm torn between the two."

I felt impelled to tender her advice along this line. I suggested to her that what she really wanted was to find the ideal man who loves her, cares for her and appreciates her, and that this love has to be mutual. "You want a man with whom you harmonize perfectly—intellectually, spiritually, and in all ways. You are now confused and full of anger toward your present husband. It is foolish to make a decision when under such a negative emotion."

I wrote a prayer for her and told her to use it and follow the lead that would come to her within the next few days. I also advised that she refrain from contacting the man she intended to marry and to just wait for inner guidance.

The prayer she used

"I know there is a principle of right action in life. I know the Life Principle in me seeks to express itself harmoniously, peacefully and joyously through me. I claim definitely that the Supreme Intelligence, which guides the cosmos and governs the planets in their courses, responds to me and guides me to make the right decision.

"I am now turning over this idea or request to the Deeper Mind within me where the Supreme Intelligence dwells, and I follow the lead which comes clearly and definitely into my conscious, reasoning mind."

She affirmed this prayer frequently during the day and, particularly, prior to sleep. On the third night she had a vision which startled her. Her deceased brother appeared to her in a vivid dream and warned her not to marry the man in San Francisco, saying that he was only going to use her, get her money, and, finally, would not marry her. The voice said, "Go back to your husband," and then the brother disappeared.

This is extrasensory perception at work. The deeper faculties of the mind could read the motives of the man she wished to marry; these faculties knew he was insincere and dishonest, and they revealed the answer to her. In other words, her subconscious mind dramatized the answer through the personality of her brother, as it knew very well she would listen to the supposed voice of her brother.

She phoned me at the Drake Hotel and said joyously, "I got my answer! I am going back to my husband." Subsequently, I learned that they have had a wonderful reconciliation. You never know how your prayers may be answered, for the ways of the subconscious are past finding out.

HOW EXTRASENSORY PERCEPTION HAS BEEN USED IN TREATMENT OF PSYCHOLOGICAL DISORDERS

In a book called *Healing the Mind*[1] by R. Connell, M.D., F.R.C.P.I., and Geraldine Cummins, a famous Irish sensitive, Dr.

---

[1] R. Connell and Geraldine Cummins, *Healing the Mind* (London, England: The Aquarian Press, 1957) .

Connell describes how he has made use of extrasensory perception in the investigation and treatment of mental disorders.

In collaboration with Geraldine Cummins, one of the most outstanding extrasensory perception operators of our time, a number of apparently hopeless cases were successfully treated. Dr. Connell, a famous medical doctor, submitted a specimen of the handwriting of mentally ill patients to Geraldine Cummins for analysis, and the following single report is taken verbatim by permission[2] from her book:

> . . . The patient was of a gentle, timid disposition, of rather poor physical development and of a somewhat worn appearance. No physical disability was determined, and her case was therefore investigated.
>
> The following report was received from an examination of a specimen of her handwriting sent to London:
>
> "The writer of this letter is highly strung and sensitive. She comes of a good family and her ancestors in some cases had remarkable qualities. But two or three of them lived hard. This led to the stock becoming rather exhausted and to a sensitive nervous system in this generation.
>
> "There is certainly a tendency here to claustrophobia and there are other fears latent in this woman's subconscious mind. She has inherited from her people, who were gentlefolk, a certain timidity due to the fact that some of them lived in the country a rather isolated life. But the fundamental cause of this lady's fear when in a confined space may be traced back perhaps two hundred years. One of her ancestors, possibly on the mother's side, owned a house and land in the country. This man was a fine character in his own way. But it seems that during troubled times a band of wild men—either tenants or people who came from the hills—one night broke suddenly into this man's house and set it alight. The wife of the owner of the house was in the first months of carrying a child. Only with difficulty did she make her escape. Indeed, she was caught in a small room that rapidly filled with smoke. She awoke to the smell of burning and to the shouts of rough men. Terrified, she perceived the smoke creeping about the room, becoming thicker and thicker. She got up

---

2 Permission granted by the Authors.

and tried to reach the door. Great waves of smoke came in. Half suffocated, she struggled forward to the threshold, where she collapsed in a faint on the floor.

"Her husband, at the risk of his life, rescued her, and after a while she revived in the cold night air. But she caught pneumonia from exposure in that bitter night, and during her delirium kept seeing the images of that room filling up with smoke, and went through again and again in her fever the agony of terror experienced in those few minutes. Slowly she recovered her health. But the fear of being shut up and trapped in a small room was, during that period of illness, transmitted to the child she was carrying.

"Her experience in that fire became a part of the race-memory of that family. When the incident of the burning of the house in that lonely countryside was forgotten consciously by the descendants of this unfortunate woman it still remained as a well-marked recollection engraven on the unconscious mind of the race. Some of the family were not affected by it, others less robust developed certain weaknesses of a nervous character.

"Physically the patient whose handwriting I am sensing is still rather run down. She ought to get out into the open air, take plenty of regular exercise and find an interest or interests of an absorbing character.

"As it occurred such a long time ago and has not been strengthened since by similar terrible shocks to her direct ancestors, it is not a pronounced thing. It has therefore no great hold. She ought to say aloud to herself at night just before she falls asleep, 'My mind is the ruler of my body. Nothing can make me afraid. I am at peace and happy in any small room or confined space.'

"The original cause of her fear—that shock to her ancestor when she was in a delicate condition—has no power over the patient when she is really physically fit and has some interesting and absorbing occupation for her mind.

"Try also to instil into Miss J. more confidence, more belief in herself. She is too diffident and distrusts her own powers.

"Let her try to assert herself and believe in herself, for she has plenty of innate capacity and intelligence. But lack of confidence, which is clearly a fault in her, greatly hinders her in life.

"Do not tell the patient the following. There is a decidedly unstable heredity, so a cure will probably take a little time and her medical attendant must watch her, and be careful lest nervous symptoms of another character break out. On the other hand, if she faithfully follows his directions heredity should be conquered."

EXTRASENSORY PERCEPTION MANIFESTED AS CLAIRAUDIENCE

A doctor friend of mine told me that invariably whenever she has an important decision to make, she hears distinctly an inner voice, which she obeys implicitly. She states that it is an oral, subconscious voice which she hears clearly either in her office or in the company of her friends. No one else hears the voice; therefore, undoubtedly, it is a subliminal uprush responding to her deep, abiding faith in inner guidance. This inner voice says, "Yes" when giving its approval and, "No" when it disapproves.

She says the inner voice is always right. This doctor has, over a period of time, conditioned her mind to believe that God is guiding her in all ways. Now she is experiencing the automatic response of her deeper mind when she needs an answer.

Clairaudience in history

Socrates openly admitted that he was constantly directed and guided by his "daemon," which he characterized as an inner, monitory voice to which he listened and obeyed. This inner voice told him what not to do and when it did not speak to him, he regarded its silence as tacit consent. In Plato's *Dialogues,* we read that this "daemon," or intuitive voice, gave Socrates extraordinary knowledge overshadowing his five senses.

Another striking instance of clairaudience is that of Joan of Arc, the remarkable visionary heroine of France. History informs us that she depended completely upon the direct messages or "voices" of her subconscious mind. Outstanding historians have investigated her extraordinary exploits down through the centuries. The conclusion of many parapsychologists and others is that she was, undoubtedly, clairvoyant and clairaudient.

One of the unique examples of her clairvoyant powers was

demonstrated when she was a young girl living in Domremy. She made known publicly that there was a sword buried behind the altar of Saint Catherine's Church at Fierbois. She had never seen the church. A man dug up the ground near the altar and found the sword exactly as she had announced.

HOW EXTRASENSORY PERCEPTION POWERS
FOUND A MISSING RECEIPT

A few weeks ago, a man telephoned me from New Orleans, Louisiana, and said that he was absolutely sure that his wife, prior to her death, had paid $2,500 in cash for a platinum watch, which was her gift to him on their golden wedding anniversay, for she had shown him the receipt. He was now being pressed for payment. He insisted to the jeweler that his wife had paid and had a receipt. The jeweler was adamant. He claimed it was charged and showed him the entry in his book.

The man searched his house thoroughly, yet failed to find the receipted bill. He said to me, "Can you help me? I have read your book *The Power of Your Subconscious Mind*,[3] and I read where a will was discovered through the power of the subconscious."

I told him that I would ask the Infinite Intelligence within to reveal the answer to him and that he would be led to it. I suggested that, likewise, he should affirm boldly and believe that Infinite Intelligence knows all things, and It knows where the receipt is and reveals it to him in Divine order.

After about a week, he wrote to me and said that while asleep one night, a person resembling an ancient sage appeared to him and pointed to a certain page in the Book of Isaiah. He saw clearly the receipted bill. He awoke suddenly and rushed to his library. He opened the Bible to the page he saw in his dream, and there was the receipt. His infinite subconscious mind provided him with the answer that transcended the power of his conscious mind.

HOW TO LET EXTRASENSORY PERCEPTION
FUNCTION FOR YOU

You have heard the wisdom of "sleep on it." This means that when your conscious mind is stilled and you focus your attention

---

[3] Joseph Murphy, *The Power of Your Subconscious Mind* (Englewood Cliffs, N.J.: Prentice-Hall, Inc., 1963).

on the solution or answer that you are seeking, the deeper mind, full of wisdom, power and Infinite Intelligence, will respond to you and solve your problem.

If you have lost something and you have searched everywhere for it, cease fretting and fussing about it, relax, let go, turn your request over to your subconscious mind and talk to it as follows: "Infinite Intelligence within my subconscious mind knows all things. It knows where this thing is and reveals it to me clearly and distinctly. I am Divinely led to it. I trust my deeper mind implicitly. I let go and relax."

When you relax, let go, become detached and preoccupied about something else, the extrasensory perception faculties of your subconscious mind will lead you directly to the thing that you lost. You may see it clairvoyantly in a dream or be led directly to where it is.

It is written, . . . *God giveth his beloved in sleep* (Ps. 127:2). We all have a wonderful legacy in these commanding words!

POINTS TO RECALL IN THIS CHAPTER

1. All of us have the powers of extrasensory perception, but in many these powers are suppressed and inhibited. Over the years they have atrophied through neglect.
2. Many people acquire specific data and information through ESP which they could not possibly receive through their ordinary five senses.
3. Your subconscious mind already knows the winner of a contest or race and can reveal it to you.
4. Professor Rhine of Duke University has gathered an enormous amount of data on telepathy, clairvoyance, clairaudience, precognition, retrocognition and telekinesis, proving the paranormal power of the mind.
5. Extra perception faculties in some young children enable them to see a funeral procession and the people in it before the funeral takes place. This could be a telepathic communication from the loved one to the child plus the precognitive faculty of the child in operation.
6. Emanuel Swedenborg had a real clairvoyant vision of a raging fire in Stockholm while he was wide awake and conversing with a group of scientists in Göteborg 250 miles away.

7. You may, through ESP, intuitively sense what is wrong with a person, enabling you to help that person reach a decision resulting in right action.

8. An outstanding Irish parapsychologist can touch a letter or a pen of a sick person given to her by the patient's doctor, and then accurately reveal the hidden complexes and fears behind his mental disturbance through ESP developed to a high degree.

9. Many people have developed the extrasensory perception faculty of clairaudience, wherein they hear an inner voice announcing approval or disapproval of their decisions. The voice is from the Supreme Intelligence within each person, which always acts for the best welfare of man.

10. Your extrasensory perception faculty can reveal to you the whereabouts of a lost article: It may dramatize the answer in a dream or show you exactly where the article lies hidden; or you may hear a voice in your sleep telling you to go someplace or do something to find it.

11. You can develop your extrasensory perception faculties and grow wiser every day by conveying these ideas to your subconscious mind (the seat of all extrasensory perception).

NINE

How the Secret Power of Self-Mastery Pays Fabulous Dividends

In the eleventh chapter of Mark, 23rd verse, we read, *For verily I say unto you, That whosoever shall say unto this mountain, Be thou removed, and be thou cast into the sea; and shall not doubt in his heart, but shall believe that those things which he saith shall come to pass; he shall have whatsoever he saith.*

The truth of these words will never let you down but will supply you with infinite power for perfect living. The mountain spoken of in the Bible stands for the difficulties, challenges and problems confronting you. They may seem overwhelming and overpowering, but if you have faith in the infinite power and do not doubt it, you will affirm boldly the following prayer:

"Be thou gone. I will overcome this challenge through the infinite power. This problem is Divinely outmatched. I will grapple with it courageously knowing that all the power, wisdom and strength necessary will be given to me. I have unquestioning faith that God knows the answer and I am one with God. God reveals to me the way out, the happy ending. I walk in that assumption and as I do, I know the mountain will disappear—will be gone out of sight, dissolved in the light of God's love. I believe this; I accept it wholeheartedly; it is so."

HOW A YOUNG AND DISCOURAGED WOMAN DEVELOPED SELF-MASTERY

A few years ago while speaking in Honolulu, a young Japanese woman suffering from discouragement and acute depression

87

visited me. She was only thirty years of age and had had extensive surgery, including the removal of a breast, as well as undergoing a hysterectomy. She said, "I'm no longer a woman. I can't give birth to children and nobody wants me." Quoting Emerson, I said to her, "You are an organ of God and God hath need of you where you are; otherwise you would not be here."

I pointed out to her that throughout life we meet with discouragement and setbacks and that there is no gainsaying the fact that trials and difficulties come to all of us, but that we have an infinite power within us which gives us power over discouragement and depression and that the joy is in overcoming and mastering any situation.

Then I suggested that the quickest way in the world for her to overcome her depression was to give of her talents, love, kindness and abilities wholeheartedly to others. In that way she would get rid of her self-absorption, self-pity and self-condemnation. I suggested that inasmuch as she was a nurse, she should go back to nursing and devote herself to giving better service to others, pouring out God's healing love on all her patients and giving more of her Divine self to others. I reminded her that the self-centered person is rarely happy and that the secret of a full life is in giving more of life, love, joy and happiness to others.

I advised her also to read the 42nd Psalm out loud several times daily savoring the words as she would a morsel of delicious food. I said I did not mean mumbling the words or idle affirmations but that I wanted her to feel and sense the magnificent truths contained therein, thereby establishing a deep, fundamental sense of oneness with God whereby her mind and heart would become transformed by the infinite power within her.

How she practiced the presence of God

She followed my suggestion and went back to nursing, pouring out grace, love and encouragement to all her patients and telling them of the infinite power of God to heal and kindle their faith. She wrote me, saying that in two years she has never lost a patient to Death. She prays for every patient under her care stating, "God is Life and His Life, Love and Power are now being manifested in

Mr. or Mrs. ———." This is her constant prayer for those under her care. This is the practice of the presence of God, because it is the constant practice of harmony, health, peace, joy, love and wholeness for each person.

Her triumphant victory

On a Christmas Day, I had the joy of performing a marriage ceremony in my home joining this nurse and the doctor who had operated on her, in the vows of holy matrimony. After the ceremony was over, her doctor husband said, "She is more than a nurse. She is an angel of mercy." He saw the inner radiance and the beauty of her soul. Emerson wrote, "Rings and jewels are not gifts. The only gift is a portion of thyself."

The following is the Psalm that stirred up the gift of God:

As the hart panteth after the water brooks, so panteth my soul after thee, O God.

My soul thirsteth for God, for the living God: when shall I come and appear before God?

My tears have been my meat day and night, while they continually say unto me, Where is thy God?

When I remember these things, I pour out my soul in me; for I had gone with the multitude, I went with them to the house of God, with the voice of joy and praise, with a multitude that kept holyday.

Why art thou cast down, O my soul? and why art thou disquieted in me? hope thou in God: for I shall yet praise him for the help of his countenance.

O my God, my soul is cast down within me: therefore will I remember thee from the land of Jordan, and of the Hermonites, from the hill Mizar.

Deep calleth unto deep at the noise of thy waterspouts: all thy waves and thy billows are gone over me.

Yet the Lord will command his loving kindness in the daytime, and in the night his song shall be with me, and my prayer unto the God of my life.

I will say unto God my rock, Why hast thou forgotten me? why go I mourning because of the oppression of the enemy?

As with a sword in my bones, mine enemies reproach me; while they say daily unto me, Where is thy God?

Why art thou cast down, O my soul? and why art thou disquieted within me? hope thou in God: for I shall yet praise him, who is the health of my countenance, and my God. (Ps. 42)

HOW TO APPLY SELF-MASTERY IN YOUR LIFE FOR RICHEST BLESSINGS

Some time ago I interviewed a woman who had been in the hospital for about two months suffering from what she called a nervous breakdown and bleeding ulcers. Her trouble was basically emotional. She said her husband was peculiar; he gave her forty dollars a week to run the house and buy food for two children, and then wondered where all the money went. He would not permit her to go to church because he felt that all religions were just "rackets." She loved to play music, but he wouldn't allow a piano at home.

She complied with his distorted, twisted, morbid ideas, thereby frustrating her own innate desires, talents and capacities. She deeply resented her husband, and her suppressed rage and frustration brought on her nervous collapse and ulcers. Her husband was playing havoc with her emotions because of his stupid, selfish, callous opposition to her ideas and values of life.

How the explanation was the cure

I explained to this talented woman that marriage is not a license to browbeat, intimidate and suppress the aspirations and personality of the other. I pointed out to her that in marriage there must be mutual love, freedom and respect and that one must cease being timid, dependent, fearful and subservient. She must become psychologically and spiritually mature and cease suppressing her personality.

In talking with both the husband and the wife, I suggested that each one cease being a scavenger, i.e., dwelling on each other's shortcomings, weaknesses and foibles, but instead, begin to see the good in each other and the wonderful qualities which they ad-

mired in each other when they married. The husband was quick
to see that the resentment and suppressed rage of his wife was the
cause of her crackups and hospitalization. They arrived at a plan
whereby the wife could express herself musically and socially.
They also agreed to open a joint checking account based on
mutual love, trust and confidence.

Here is the pattern of prayer I suggested for the husband:
"From now on I will cease trying to change my wife's personality.
I do not want her to be a second edition of myself, neither do I
want her to submerge her talents or personality. I radiate love,
peace and goodwill to her. My sincere prayer is that the Infinite
Intelligence within her rules, guides and directs her in all ways
and that Divine love flows through her mind and body at all times.
God's peace floods her mind constantly. I exalt God in the midst of
her. I claim she is happy, joyous, healthy and Divinely expressed. I
know that my thought is my prayer and that my thoughts execute
themselves. I know also that prayer is a habit, and as I continue
thinking habitually along these lines I will become a loving, kind
and understanding husband. Whenever I think of my wife I will
silently affirm, 'God loves and cares for you.' "

Prayer patterns for
the wife to follow

"I saw wonderful qualities in my husband when I married him.
These qualities are still there, and from now on I will identify
with his fine qualities and not with his shortcomings. I know, feel
and claim the Infinite Intelligence leads, guides and directs him in
all ways. Regularly and systematically I exalt God in the midst of
him. Divine law and order govern his activities. Divine peace fills
his soul. Divine love flows through his thoughts, words and deeds
toward me and the children. God loves him and cares for him. He
is a tremendous success and God prospers him. He is inspired from
On High. I know that all these thoughts reiterated regularly and
systematically by me find their way to my subconscious mind; and,
like seeds, they come forth after their kind. Whenever I think of
my husband I will immediately affirm, 'God in me salutes the God
in you.' "

How persistence pays dividends
and brings mastery

Both the husband and wife remained faithful to their agreement and prayer life. They knew that to believe something is to bring it to pass. Believe is made up of two words, "be alive." The old English meaning of the word is to "live in the state of being," which means making it real in your life. At the end of about a month, I received a phone call from the wife saying, "I became alive (believed) to these truths which you wrote out for me. They are registered in my heart (subconscious mind)." The husband added, "I am now master over my thoughts, emotions and reactions, and so is my wife. Self-mastery is a real thing in our lives." They discovered that the infinite power for perfect living is always within themselves.

HOW A DISCOURAGED YOUNG MAN GAINED
SELF-ESTEEM AND RECOGNITION

A young man complained to me that he is constantly slighted in social gatherings and is also passed over for promotion in his organization. He added that he frequently entertains in his home, but that he is never invited as a guest to the homes of his associates and others whom he has entertained. There was a deep and violent animus in his heart toward everyone.

While this well educated young man conferred with me and while discussing his childhood and home environment, he informed me that he had been brought up by a puritanical New England father. His mother had died at his birth. His father, who was somewhat tyrannical and despotic, frequently said to his son, "You're no good. You will never amount to anything. You are stupid. Why aren't you smart like your brother? I am ashamed of your school record." I discovered that this man actually hated his father. He grew up with a rejection complex and unconsciously felt unacceptable to people. To use a vernacular expression, he had a psychic boil and was terribly touchy in the field of human relations. This was accompanied by a subjective expectation and fear of being rejected by others, either by rude affront or by what is commonly called "the brush-off."

How his negative complexes were eliminated

I pointed out to him that in my estimation he was constantly fearing slights and rejection; furthermore, he was projecting his animosity and resentment of his father onto others. Compulsively he wanted to be disparaged, rejected or dismissed by someone's manner, attitude, comment or by what seemed to be a greater interest in others. I explained to him the law of his mind and gave him a copy of *The Power of Your Subconscious Mind.*[1] In the meantime I gave him a very practical plan for overcoming his rejection complex and assuming mastery over his life.

The practical step-by-step plan

The first step in solving a problem of this type is to realize that no matter what the past experiences may have been, these can be completely eradicated by feeding the subconscious mind with eternal verities and life-giving patterns of thought. Since the subconscious mind is amenable to suggestion and controlled by the conscious mind, all negative patterns, complexes, fears and inferiorities can be expunged. These are the life-giving patterns:

"I recognize these truths to be true. I am a son of the Living God. God indwells me and is my real self. From this moment forward I will love God within me. Love means to honor, respect, give allegiance to and be loyal to the only Presence and the only Power. From now on I respect the Divinity which shapes my ends. This God-Presence within me created me, sustains me and is the Life-Principle within me. The Bible says, *Love thy neighbor as thyself* (Lev. 19:18). The neighbor is the closest thing to me, or, Closer is He than breathing; nearer than hands and feet. Every conscious moment of the day I honor, exalt, glorify and have a healthy and reverent respect for the Divine Presence within me. I know that as I exalt and have a healthy and wholesome respect for

---

1 Joseph Murphy, *The Power of Your Subconscious Mind* (Englewood Cliffs, N.J.: Prentice-Hall, Inc., 1963).

the God-Self within me, I will automatically respect and love the God in the other person. Whenever I am prone to criticize or find fault with myself, I will immediately affirm, 'I honor, love and exalt the God-Presence within me, and I love the Self of me more and more every day.' I know I cannot love and respect others until I first love, honor, respect and pay loyalty and devotion to my real Self—God—in the midst of me, which is mighty to heal. Honoring God within myself, I will honor the dignity and Divine royalty of all men. I know these truths, when repeated feelingly, knowingly and believingly, enter into my subconscious mind; and I am subconsciously compelled to express these truths, as the nature of my subconscious mind is compulsion. Whatever is impressed, I am compelled to express. I believe this implicitly. It is wonderful!"

The second step is to reiterate these truths frequently three or four times a day at special periods in order to establish a habit of constructive thinking.

The third step is never to condemn, demean or demote yourself. The moment a thought comes to your mind such as, "I'm no good," "a jinx is following me," "I'm unwanted" or "I'm nobody," immediately reverse the thought by saying, "I exalt God in the midst of me."

The fourth step is to imagine yourself mingling with your associates in a friendly, amiable and affable manner. Imagine and hear your superiors congratulating you on a job well done. Imagine you are being welcomed and accepted graciously in the homes of your friends. Above all, believe in your image and in its reality.

The fifth step is to realize and know that whatever you habitually think upon and image must come to pass, for that which is impressed on your subconscious mind must be expressed on the screen of space as experiences, conditions and events.

This young man diligently followed the above procedure, knowing what he was doing and why he was doing it. Having a knowledge of the way his subconscious mind worked, he gained confidence daily in his technique and application. Gradually he succeeded in cleansing his subconscious of all the early psychic traumas. He is now welcomed in the homes of his associates and has been entertained by the president and vice-president of his organization. Since adopting these psychological procedures he has received two promotions and is now executive vice-president of his bank. He knows that application of the cosmic power within him brings self-mastery over the past or conditions, experiences and events. It is done unto you as you believe.

HOW COMPLETE MARITAL UNHAPPINESS WAS OVERCOME

Recently I received a letter from a woman in Texas:

> Dear Dr. Murphy: I read your book *The Cosmic Power Within You,*[2] from which I received great help. I would like your advice on my problem. My husband is constantly criticizing me using abusive, sarcastic and vitriolic language. The mendacity of my husband makes it impossible for me to believe anything he says. He sleeps in a separate room and there is no marital intimacy. No matter what kind of community work I do, he finds fault. In the last five years we have had no guests in our home. I am full of antipathy toward my husband. I am afraid I am beginning to hate him. I have left him twice. We have had spiritual counseling, as well as psychological help and legal advice. I can't communicate with him. What shall I do?

My reply was as follows:

> Dear _____: You can't afford to resent or hate anybody in the world. Such feelings or attitudes are mental poisons which debilitate the entire mentality and rob you of peace, harmony, health, and good judgment. They corrode your soul and leave you a physical and mental wreck. You are the only thinker in your world and you are responsible for the way you think about your husband—he is not. My suggestion to you is that you stop trying to communicate with him and to surrender him to God completely, lock, stock and barrel. It is wrong to live a lie. It is better to break up a lie than to live it. There is a time in our experience when, having done everything we can to solve a problem, we should follow the injunction of Paul, "Having done all, I stand," i.e., you stand on the Cosmic Wisdom within you to solve the problem. You

---

2 Joseph Murphy, *The Cosmic Power Within You* (West Nyack, N.Y.: Parker Publishing Company, Inc., 1968).

have visited psychologists, lawyers and pastors, obviously in a spirit of goodwill, to bring about a healing; but, apparently, there is no solution in sight. Turn your mind to constructive pursuits and adopt a new attitude toward your husband, such as, "None of these things moves me."

Here is a pattern of prayer, which, when followed by you, will bring results, for the Cosmic Power never fails:

"I surrender my husband to God. God made him and sustains him. God reveals to him his true place in life where he is Divinely happy and Divinely blessed. The Cosmic Wisdom reveals to him the perfect plan and shows him the way he should go. The Cosmic Power flows through him as love, peace, harmony, joy and right action. I am Divinely guided to do the right thing and to make the right decision. I know that what is right action for me is right action for my husband; also, I know that what blesses one blesses all. Whenever I think of my husband, and no matter what he says or does, all I do is to affirm knowingly and feelingly, 'I have surrendered you to God.' I am at peace about everything, and I wish for my husband all the blessings of life."

I recommended that she cultivate a constructive life of her own, expressing her talents and continuing in community projects. I advised her to remain faithful to the specific prayer, explaining to her that these God-like thoughts would cleanse her subconscious mind of all resentment and other negative and destructive poison pockets lodged in her deeper mind. This would be done in the same way as clean water drop by drop will, if we persist, cleanse a pail of dirty water so that we will have clean water to drink. You can, of course, turn the hose on a pail of dirty water and get clean water faster. The hose, figuratively speaking, would be a transfusion of Divine love and goodwill into the soul, bringing about an immediate cleansing. However, a gradual cleansing process is the usual procedure.

An interesting denouement

The sequel to the above prayer process is interesting, as the following letter reveals:

Dear Dr. Murphy: I am deeply grateful for your letter, advice and prayer technique, which I have followed faithfully. When he became sarcastic and poured forth expletives and invectives, I blessed him by silently affirming, "I surrender you to God." I became interested in hospital and community work and have made many friends the last six weeks since I started praying. My husband asked for a divorce last week, to which I gladly agreed. We have already made a property settlement which is mutually satisfactory. He is going to Reno for a divorce and plans to marry a woman whom I feel is right for him. I have fallen in love also with a childhood sweetheart of mine, whom I met in my hospital work. We are to be married as soon as I am legally free.

Truly God works in mysterious ways His wonders to perform.

POINTS TO RECALL IN THIS CHAPTER

1. Realize every problem is Divinely outmatched. The Cosmic Power which knows all and sees all is within you. Grapple with your challenge courageously and the Cosmic Wisdom will reveal to you the answer. The mountain (obstacle) will be cast into the sea (dissolved, obliterated from sight).

2. The quickest and surest way to overcome depression and discouragement is to give of your talents, love, kindness and consideration wholeheartedly to others. Perform some act of kindness for another, visit a hospital and exalt God in the midst of a sick friend, and give the other a transfusion of loving kindness.

3. A wonderful spiritual antidote to depression and self-absorption is to dwell upon the truths of the 42nd Psalm. This Psalm will lift you up and inspire you.

4. The practice of the Presence of God is the constant realization of the presence of God's peace, harmony, joy, wholeness, beauty, illumination, love and goodwill in yourself and in your neighbor.

5. Husbands and wives should identify with the good qualities in each other and with the characteristics that endeared one to the other when they got married. As they see God in each other and exalt His Presence in one another, harmony

will prevail and the marriage will grow more blessed through the years.

6. Husbands should not try to suppress the personalities of their wives, and wives should cease trying to do the same. Each is unique. A person whose personality is suppressed becomes neurotic and frustrated. Each should rejoice in the full expression of talent in the other.

7. Persistence pays great dividends. Remain faithful to your prayer process. To believe is to be alive to certain great truths which are eternal. Make them a living part of you— that is believing, and according to your belief is it done unto you.

8. When a man feels he is constantly slighted and rejected, this is invariably due to a "psychic boil" within himself wherein he expects rejection and the brush-off. The cure is to exalt constantly the God-Presence within him, which is his real self, and to fill his subconscious mind with the truths of God, which crowd out of his mind everything unlike God or the truth.

9. When you have honestly tried every conceivable way to solve a problem, and when you have sought counsel and expert advice, both spiritual and psychological, and your motivation is right, then, as Paul suggests: "Having done all, I stand." You stand firmly on the truth that the Cosmic Power within you knows the answer and will reveal the perfect solution as you completely surrender the matter to God, knowing and believing in your heart the answer will come. Then day breaks and the shadows flee away.

TEN

How to Use
Infinite Power for
Fulfilled Living

On Thanksgiving Day I flew to the Island of Kauai to mingle with the people, to visit the various towns and scenic spots, and above all to get acquainted with some of the full-blooded Hawaiians. I met a guide who introduced me to many of his friends and took me to several houses in the Island to see how they live. I found the people in the homes I visited to be happy, joyous and free. They are kind, generous, deeply spiritual and full of the music and laughter of God. I found myself looking at people who, through love of God, are living life gloriously in the spirit of Divine Liberty. In the following pages I am going to elaborate on how you too may set a pattern for victorious living.

HOW A PATTERN FOR VICTORIOUS LIVING WAS FOUND

In making a few purchases in one remote village here, I had an interesting conversation with a man who came from the mainland some years ago and who is now running a country store. He said to me that he had been an alcoholic. His wife had deserted him and had taken all the money with her (they had a joint account). He had become bitter, irascible and hateful and had found great difficulty in meshing into an organization. A friend suggested that he go to Kauai, explaining to him that it was the oldest island of the Hawaiian chain and that it basks in rare beauty, full of lush

99

foliage and floral growth. His friend told him of the deep colorful canyons, golden beaches and winding rivers, all of which captured his imagination.

How a change of heart took place

He worked in the sugar cane fields here for some months. One day he fell ill and was confined to a hospital for several weeks. Each day the Hawaiian people visited him, brought him fruit, prayed for him and showed a deep interest in his welfare. Their kindness, love and attention penetrated his heart, and he reciprocated by pouring out love, peace and goodwill to them. He became a transformed man.

A pattern for perfect living

This man's formula is very simple; it is that love will always win over hate, and goodness will always win over evil, for that is the way the universe is made. I would like to comment on what transpired psychologically and spiritually in this case. This man's heart was corroded with bitterness, self-condemnation and hatred for women. The love, kindness and prayers of his fellow workers penetrated the layers of his subconscious mind, expunging all the negative patterns lodged therein, and his heart became full of love and goodwill to all. He discovered that love is the universal solvent. His constant prayer now is, "I pour out God's love, peace and joy to every person I meet every day of my life." The more love he gives, the more he receives. It is more blessed to give than to receive.

FIVE STEPS TO LIVING LIFE GLORIOUSLY

1. Every morning when you open your eyes affirm boldly and with deep feeling and understanding, "This is the day which the Lord hath made; rejoice and be glad in it. I shall rejoice and give thanks that my life is directed by the same Eternal Wisdom which guides the planets in their courses and causes the sun to shine.

2. "I am going to live life gloriously today and every day. More

and more of God's love, light, truth and beauty are being experienced by me all day long today and every day.

3. "I am going to be of tremendous help to all those whom I contact and with whom I work, and have the time of my life doing it.

4. "I am going to be wildly enthusiastic about my work and my wonderful opportunities for service.

5. "I rejoice and give thanks that more and more of God's love, life and truth are being experienced by me every day, and more and more of God's glory is being made manifest by me."

Begin each day by affirming these miraculous truths and believe in their reality. Whatever you believe and faithfully anticipate will come to pass, and wonders will happen in your life.

HOW YOU CAN LEARN TO WALK AND TALK
WITH GOD FOR PEACE AND SERENITY

I met an extraordinary man at the Fern Grotto, where the boat crew are noted for singing the never-forgotten Hawaiian Wedding Song. He was ninety-six years of age, walked briskly and sang lustily the beautiful Hawaiian love songs on the boat taking us to the famous Grotto. After the trip he invited me to his home, which was indeed a rare experience. For dinner we had thickly sliced homemade gingerbread, papaya, apple tart, rice, broiled salmon and Kona coffee grown on one of the neighboring islands.

During dinner he told me how he had become a new man in God, and at ninety-six he certainly looked the part. His cheeks were ruddy with radiant and buoyant health; his eyes were filled with light and love; joy was all over his face. He spoke fluently English, Spanish, Chinese, Japanese and the Hawaiian languages. He regaled me with as fine a flood of native wisdom, witticisms, jokes and good humor as I had ever heard.

I was thoroughly fascinated and I finally asked him, "Tell me your secret of life and joy. You seem to be bubbling over with enthusiasm and energy." "Why shouldn't I be happy and strong?" he replied. "You see, I own the island and yet I own nothing." He added, "God possesses everything, but the whole island and all that is in it is mine to enjoy—the mountains, the rivers, the caves, the people and the rainbows. Do you know where I got this home?" he asked, and he answered himself, saying, "A grateful tourist bought it for me and gave it to me as a gift; otherwise, I wouldn't have had it."

How God healed him

He added that about sixty years ago he was dying of tuberculosis and had been given up as hopeless, but a local Kahuna (native priest) visited him and told both him and his mother that he would live and that God would heal him. The Kahuna chanted prayers, placed his hands on his throat and chest and in his native tongue called on God's healing power. At the end of about an hour's chanting, he said he was completely healed and the next day he went fishing. Since then, he said, "I've never had a pain or an ache of any kind. I have marvelous legs. I've walked all over these mountains you see. Moreover," he concluded, "I have kind, loving friends, a few dogs and goats, and this wonderful island. And I have God in my heart. Why shouldn't I be happy and strong?"

This man really walks and talks with God, and having God in his heart, he is happy every day. This wonderful man tills his land, takes care of his goats and sheep, visits the sick, attends all the festivals and sings Hawaiian love songs which touch the soul of man.

His song for health and vitality

The only prescription the Kahuna gave him was, "Sing the 100th Psalm. Morning, noon and night live with these truths in your heart and you will never again be sick." He sang it for me, and I have never in my life heard anything so moving, penetrating, lovely and soul stirring. It was like the melody of God played on your sacral plexus.

This is the Psalm of praise:

> *Make a joyful noise unto the Lord, all ye lands.*
> *Serve the Lord with gladness: come before his presence with singing.*
> *Know ye that the Lord he is God: it is he that hath made*

*us, and not we ourselves; we are his people, and the sheep of
his pasture.*

*Enter into his gates with thanksgiving, and into his courts
with praise: be thankful unto him, and bless his name.*

*For the Lord is good; his mercy is everlasting; and his truth
endureth to all generations.*

(Ps. 100:1–5)

How faith and receptivity heals

Knowing the laws of mind, you can readily see the impression
his Kahuna priest made upon him. He had absolute faith in the
powers of the Kahuna, and he believed implicitly that he would
be healed. According to his belief, his subconscious mind responded. Today, as he sings the 100th Psalm daily, his mind and
heart are lifted up in grateful acknowledgment to God; and there
is an automatic reaction of the Law bringing countless blessings in
its train.

The law of thanksgiving

A grateful heart is always close to God; and as this man gives
thanks daily for his health, abundance and security and for his
many blessings, God multiplies his good exceedingly. This is based
on the law of action and reaction, which is cosmic and universal.
The Bible says, *Draw nigh to God and He will draw nigh to you*
(Jas. 4:8). Thoreau said, "We should give thanks that we were
born." Practice singing and living the truths of the 100th Psalm.
Write these truths in your heart by repeating them slowly, lovingly, and feelingly. As you do, these ideas will find their way by
repetition to the deeper layers of your mind, and, like seeds, they
will grow after their kind. Let wonders happen in your life.

HOW A GRANDMOTHER KEEPS INSPIRED
AND ZESTFUL FOR LIFE

I chatted with a grandmother who sat next to me on the boat
trip to the famous Waimea Canyon, a gorge cut to the depth of
about 3,000 feet by the Waimea River. She was taking her two

granddaughters sightseeing. She commented on the gorgeous colorings of the cliff strata and the tropical growth covering the sides of the canyon. I might add that the shadows of the ever-changing clouds made it an unforgettable sight. This beautiful, spiritual woman told me that she is over ninety years of age and has never been sick a day in her life, the reason being, she said, "I keep prayed up." This Hawaiian woman teaches Sunday School, writes poetry, rows a boat, fishes, milks her two cows every day, talks before women's groups and is now planning a tour for twenty to Europe.

She showed me a card on which were typed the words of Tennyson: "Oh, I see the crescent promise of my spirit hath not set. Ancient founts of inspiration well through all my fancy yet." On the back of the card was this Biblical verse: *Ho, every one that thirsteth, come ye to the waters, and he that hath no money; come ye, buy, and eat; yea, come, buy wine and milk without money and without price* (Isa. 55:1).

Wine in the Bible means inspiration from On High, where the Holy Spirit flows through you energizing and vitalizing your whole being. Milk is symbolic of nourishment. Your mind needs nourishment as well as your body. Feed your mind with ideas which heal, bless, elevate, inspire and dignify your soul. Feed your mind daily on thoughts of love, peace, faith, confidence, success and Divine right action. The price you pay is attention, devotion and loyalty to these eternal verities.

Her key to joyous living

This woman found the key to an inspired and zestful life by living in her heart these two wonderful quotations until they became a living part of her. She believed what she affirmed and lived in the joyous expectancy of what she affirmed. She exuded vibrancy, joy and goodwill. She discovered that daily communion with the Father within is the answer to Cosmic Power for perfect living.

A GREAT SPIRITUAL FEAST

I visited a famous woman in the charming and exotic island of Maui. There were assembled in her home a group of distinguished people, and we discussed mental and spiritual laws from about 10:00 A.M. until 4:00 P.M. Her guests were familiar with the books *The Power of Your Subconscious Mind*[1] and *Miracle of Mind Dynamics*.[2] In the whole course of my life I have never met a more enthusiastic, happy, joyful group. Their hearts were kindled with a Divine fire. They spoke about how they overcame their problems by believing in a power greater than themselves or their conscious egos. They have talk fests on my books and listen to my recordings. They asked questions which delighted me and which showed a tremendous interest and insight into things Divine. They have discovered that the joy of living is in the contemplation of the truths of God regularly and systematically.

HAWAIIAN WISDOM AND INNER JOY

I have found that the Hawaiians are very wise people, having acquired through centuries a vast accumulation of esoteric and unwritten knowledge. One man, a native of Maui who sat next to me on the plane from Kauai to Maui, was a full-blooded Hawaiian and had knowledge of weather conditions, currents, tides, etc. He informed me that he could predict tidal waves, storms and volcanic eruptions. He knows by name all the fruits, flowers and trees in the islands and understands the curative properties of the herbs in the islands.

He has the capacity to read minds and is definitely clairvoyant. He told me where I was going, gave my name and address and had the gift of retrocognition, as he spoke most accurately of many past events in my life. To test his gift of clairvoyance, I asked him to read a letter which was in my pocket, which I had not as yet read, having forgotten all about it until that moment. He read the contents accurately, as my subsequent reading verified.

This young man has a native wisdom. He is in touch with his subconscious mind, which knows the answers to all questions. "Whenever I want to know something," he said, "I just say, 'God, you know. Tell me.' The answer always comes, because I have a friend inside." This man works in the cane fields, plays the

---

1 Joseph Murphy, *The Power of Your Subconscious Mind* (Englewood Cliffs, N.J.: Prentice-Hall, Inc., 1963).

2 Joseph Murphy, *Miracle of Mind Dynamics* (Englewood Cliffs, N.J.: Prentice-Hall, Inc., 1964).

ukulele, sings at his work and obviously is in tune with the Infinite. Truly, he has a friend inside and he has discovered the joy of the God-Presence which is his strength.

THE SEVEN-STEP MIRACLE FORMULA

During my stay in the islands I set aside one day for interviewing people who wished to consult with me at the Hotel there in Kauai. My first visitor was a man whom I had previously counseled a few years ago at the Royal Hawaiian Hotel in Honolulu. At that time he was a confirmed alcoholic and had been pronounced an inebriate and a compulsive drinker. He had had drug treatment, hypnosis and other forms of therapy. He said, "I came to thank you and will only take a few minutes of your time. You told me that I was master of the bottle and that the bottle had no power. You said to stop all alibis and excuses and to become a real man. I followed the technique you outlined. I forgave myself and others, and today I own my own store, I am married, I belong to the local church, and I have two wonderful children. I just came to thank you, that's all."

I remembered him very well and recalled talking with him in Honolulu. At that time he had just been released from the hospital where he had been undergoing treatment for alcoholism. Here are the steps which I gave him that transformed his life:

1. I fully and freely forgive myself for harboring grudges, peeves and ill will toward others. Whenever I think of others I wish for them all the blessings of life.

2. I am the king and complete master over my thoughts, words, actions, emotions and reactions. I am absolute monarch over my conceptive realm.

3. I desire to become completely free from this habit. I mean this and I am absolutely sincere. I know that when my desire to give it up is greater than my desire to continue, I am 60 per cent healed already.

4. I have made my decision and I know that according to my decision is it done unto me. My subconscious mind knows I am sincere.

5. I now use my imagination correctly. I know my power to

image is the primal force of man and the greatest of all my faculties. Three times a day for three or four minutes I will run a motion picture in my mind wherein I see my mother congratulating me on my perfect health and freedom. I hear her voice and feel her embrace, and I enter into the joy of it all. Whenever I am tempted, I instantaneously flash on this mental movie in my mind. I know my mental picture is backed up by the power of God.

6. I know what I am doing and why I am doing it. I know that according to my belief is it done unto me. I know that to believe is to accept something as true. I know my desire is true, my mental image is real and the power that backs me up is of God. I know all the power of God is directed at the focal point of my attention.

7. I am now free and I give thanks.

I have given this seven-step miracle formula to many alcoholics, victims of LSD and marijuana, dope addicts, etc. You can overcome any negative habit by following these simple principles. This man is happy, joyous, bubbling over with the élan of life. I have attended a dinner at his home where coconut palms rattled conversationally in vagrant breezes; ocean waves swished nearby and receded, leaving foam in the sand; and bright tropical flowers surrounded us on all sides. The iced papaya and lemon was as sweet as the nectar of the gods. And the poi, their staple dish, was deliciously flavored with nutmeg and cinnamon. Beauty, serenity and the joy of living were present in the entire atmosphere of the home. He and his family prayed before and after dinner giving thanks for all their blessings, and Hawaiian love songs and music filled his home. Truly, I had entered into what we call infinite power for perfect living.

HOW TO ACQUIRE THE JOY OF LIVING

I have been in correspondence with a young girl on this island whom I will call Mary. She has been studying the book *The Power of Your Subconscious Mind*,[3] which I sent her some months ago. In her original letter to me at my home in Beverly Hills, she said she was full of abnormal fear and was a tied-up personality.

---

3 Joseph Murphy, *The Power of Your Subconscious Mind* (Englewood Cliffs, N.J.: Prentice-Hall, Inc., 1963).

She had broken her engagement to a young man, and he had retaliated by informing her that a Kahuna had cursed her. She lived in constant fear. I wrote to her explaining that there is only One Power, and that this Power moves as unity and harmony in the world; that God is Spirit, One and Indivisible; and that one part of Spirit could not be antagonistic to another part of Spirit; therefore, there was nothing to fear. I wrote out a spiritual technique for her to follow, which would banish all fear.

In my interview with her today, I find a radiant personality, a young woman exuding vibrancy, bubbling over with enthusiasm and joy, and on fire with new ideas for the island. She said, "I followed your instructions to the letter and I am transformed by an inner light."

The following is the spiritual regimen she practiced several times daily, as suggested in my letter to her:

"God is all there is. One with God is a majority. *If God be for me who can be against me?* (Rom. 8:31) I know and believe God is the Living Spirit Almighty—the Ever-Living One, the All-Wise One—and there is no power to challenge God. I know and accept completely that when my thoughts are God's thoughts, God's power is with my thoughts of good. I know I cannot receive what I cannot give, and I give out thoughts of love, peace, light and goodwill to my ex-boyfriend and all those connected with him. I am immunized and God-intoxicated, and I am always surrounded by the sacred circle of God's love. The whole armor of God surrounds me and enfolds me. I am Divinely guided and directed, and I enter into the joy of living. *In thy presence is fulness of joy; at thy right hand there are pleasures for evermore* (Ps. 16:11)."

She practiced repeating these truths regularly and systematically for about ten minutes morning, afternoon and night, knowing, believing and understanding that as she affirmed these truths they would gradually sink into her subconscious mind by a process of spiritual osmosis and come forth as freedom, inner peace, a sense of security, confidence and protection. She knew she was applying a law of mind which never fails. In ten days' time all fear vanished. Now she has a wonderful position here in the island. She introduced me to her new fiancé, and his comment was, "She is the joy of my life." This young woman who had been practically petrified by fear of a supposed curse is now out-flowing, giving of her talents, and has entered into the joy of living.

THE MEANING OF KAHUNA

Most of the Hawaiian people here and in the other islands claim that there are no more Kahunas, and most of the Hawaiians are unwilling to talk about them. There is, however, the type called the white Kahuna, meaning a man who practices white magic, or casts good spells by his incantations and esoteric knowledge. One of my Hawaiian guides explained to me that these Kahunas were trained from early childhood by their elders, who subjected them to severe discipline and secrecy. Many of them are highly respected for their healing powers through what we would call today knowledge of the subconscious mind. They have, also, a knowledge of the curative properties of certain herbs and plants. My guide, who seemed more willing than others to discuss the subject, pointed out that some of the Kahunas are greatly feared as Kahuna anaanas, i.e., those who dealt with death or black magic.

The above-mentioned lady learned that the threats, negative suggestions and statements of others have absolutely no power to create the things they suggest. You are the only thinker in your universe. It is your thought that is creative. Think good and good follows; think evil and evil follows. Join with God. When your thoughts are God's thoughts, God's Power is with your thoughts of good. Remember, "One with God is a majority," and *If God be for me, who can be against me?* (Rom. 8:31)

POINTS TO RECALL IN THIS CHAPTER

1. Love of God, which means the love of or emotional attachment to all things good, will enable you to live life gloriously.
2. Love, kindness and goodwill will melt the ice in the other person's heart and will bring a reciprocal action from the person to whom it is directed. Love is the universal solvent.
3. When you open your eyes in the morning affirm gladly, "This is the day which the Lord hath made for me. I will rejoice and be glad in it. I give thanks that my life is directed by the same Wisdom that guides the planets in their courses and causes the sun to shine." Believe in

God's guidance and wonders will happen in your life.

4. Realize that age is not the flight of years. It is the dawn of wisdom in your mind. God possesses all things and the whole world was here when you were born. Let the joy of the Lord be your strength.

5. Live with the great truths of the 100th Psalm. It is a thanksgiving ode to God. Sing these truths into your soul until they become an integral part of you, just as bread digested becomes part of your bloodstream.

6. A grateful heart is always close to God. The Bible says, *Draw nigh to God and He will draw nigh to you* (Jas. 4:8).

7. You can feel inspired and zestful all your life. Every morning call upon God and He will answer you.

8. You can discover the joy of living in contemplation of the truths of God regularly and systematically. You become what you contemplate.

9. The powers of clairvoyance, precognition and telepathy are within you. As you grow in wisdom, you will begin to tap the infinite reservoir within you, and these latent faculties will become active in your life.

10. You cannot receive what you cannot give. This is a law of mind. Give love, joy and goodwill to all. The more you give the more blessings come to you.

11. You are the only thinker in your universe. There is nothing in God's universe to fear. *I will fear no evil for Thou art with me* (Ps. 23:4). "One with God is a majority." *If God be for me who can be against me?* (Rom. 8:31)

ELEVEN

How to Get the Infinite Power on Your Side

One of the keys to the understanding of life is to realize that everything comes in pairs. All action consists of the interworking of opposites. A combination of male and female life forces created the universe. Emerson once said, "Polarity, or action and reaction, we meet in every part of nature." We have spirit and matter, male and female, positive and negative, sickness and health, love and hatred, night and day, heat and cold, in and out, sweet and sour, up and down, north and south, subjective and objective, motion and rest, yes and no, success and failure, sadness and gladness, etc. Spirit and matter are but aspects of the One Reality. Matter is spirit reduced to the point of visibility. Matter is the lowest degree of spirit and spirit is the highest degree of matter. These opposites in life are manifestations of the One Being and are necessary to experience life.

In the absolute state there is no differentiation, contrast or established relationship. It subsists in a state of oneness. When the Absolute became relative, i.e., when God created the universe, He created the opposites so that we might experience sensation and function and the sense of being alive. We must have feeling and sensibility in order to be aware of being alive. We know by contrast the difference between heat and cold, height and depth, length and breadth, sweet and sour, depression and elation, male and female, and subjective and objective. All these opposites are halves of the One Being which is whole, perfect and indivisible.

HOW THOUGHTS COME IN PAIRS

A young boy, aged twelve, who listens to my morning radio program, told his mother that he was going to visit his uncle in Australia during school vacation. His thought of going was very strong, but he had another thought which said, "Mom won't let me go." His mother had said, "It's impossible. We don't have the money and your father can't possibly afford it. You're dreaming."

Her son said, however, that he heard on my radio program that if you desired to do something and believed that the Creative Intelligence within you would bring it to pass, your prayer would be answered. His mother said, "Go ahead and pray." This boy who had been reading extensively about Australia and New Zealand had an uncle in Australia who owned a big ranch. He prayed as follows:

"God opens up the way for Dad, Mom and myself to go to Australia during vacation. I believe this and God takes over now." When the thought that his parents didn't have the money to go came to his mind, he would affirm, "God opens up the way." His thoughts came in pairs, but he gave attention to the constructive thought and the negative thought died away.

How he traveled astrally

One night he had a dream wherein he found himself on his uncle's ranch in New South Wales, viewing thousands of sheep, and meeting his uncle and cousins. When he awakened the next morning, he described the entire scene to his mother, much to her amazement. The same day a cablegram came from his uncle inviting the three of them to his ranch and offering to defray their expenses both ways. They accepted.

The boy's intense desire to visit his uncle acted on his subconscious mind as a command while asleep; and, using his fourth-dimensional body, he traveled astrally to the ranch. The boy told me that what he observed when he arrived at the ranch with his parents coincided exactly with what he saw in his astral projection while asleep. Thus, it was done unto him as he believed.

HOW A FEAR OF A SECOND MARRIAGE
WAS DESTROYED

A young woman said to me, "I desire to get married, but the thought of fear comes into my mind that I will attract the wrong man and repeat the same mistake as in my previous marriage." Fear warred with her desire, and her fear thought seemed to be the dominant one. I explained to her that everything comes in pairs. For example, if one thinks of health, the thought of sickness comes to the mind; if one thinks of wealth, the thought of poverty comes to the mind; if we speak of the good heart, we think of the bad heart; and so on.

I explained to her that the way to overcome the negative thought was to take her attention completely away from the fear thought and lift her mind above the opposition by contemplating the joyous fulfillment of her marriage to the right man.

The technique used for
joyous fulfillment

"I know there is only One Almighty Power, which knows no opposition. There is nothing to oppose, challenge or vitiate it. It is invulnerable and invincible, and I now decree that I attract the right man who blends with me spiritually, mentally and physically. I give my whole-hearted attention to this idea in my mind trusting the law of my subconscious to bring it to pass." When the fear thought came into her mind, she affirmed, "God is taking care of my request." After a few days the fear thought lost all momentum and died away. She made her ideal live by feeding and nourishing it with faith and confidence in her mind.

How she met her future
husband's fourth-dimensional
(astral) body

Every night of your life when you go to sleep you go to the next dimension of life, which is called the *fourth dimension* and which interpenetrates this plane. Shortly after she began her prayer technique, she had a vivid dream in which I was performing her marriage ceremony in my home. She perceived her future husband and heard me pronounce his name and ask him to repeat the vows of the marriage ceremony. It was all very vivid and real. She felt herself to be in my home and touched the statue of Buddha, as well as the paintings on the walls.

With great joy and happiness she awakened and phoned me, telling me what had happened in her sleep. She described the room where I perform marriage ceremonies in minute detail. I explained to her that, while asleep, she had traveled to my home in her fourth-dimensional (astral) body, which is supercharged with electrons, rarefied and attenuated, vibrating at tremendous speed, and capable of penetrating walls, etc. I pointed out to her that, undoubtedly, the marriage had already taken place in the next dimension of mind and that her own conviction and inner realization would bring it to pass.

The final touch to her astral journey

This young lady, who works as a secretary for a large organization, was invited to a home by the wife of one of the executives. Her hostess introduced her to her son, who happened to be the man she saw in her dream! He said to her, "I have seen you before." He proceeded to tell her about his dream of the marriage ceremony by a strange minister in a private home, both of which he had never seen before. They had had identical dreams, and subsequently the author performed the marriage ceremony, which coincided in every detail with this combined, four-dimensional experience.

My explanation is that this young lady, thinking with interest about the type of man she wished to marry, inscribed the idea on her subconscious mind, which, in turn, dramatized its contents in a fourth-dimensional rehearsal, as everything that happens objectively must first take place subjectively. Infinite Intelligence in her subconscious mind brought them together fourth dimensionally as well as third dimensionally.

WHY YOU ARE YOUR OWN LEGISLATOR IN HAVING GOOD OR FRUSTRATING EXPERIENCES

Your habitual thoughts, conceptions and opinions evoke certain emotions within you which impress your subconscious mind, and you automatically repeat these patterns in your life experience like an automaton or some sort of a mechanical robot. The law of your mind is such that whatever you impress on your subconscious mind is made manifest as experience, conditions and events in your life. Your thoughts (good or bad) are your mental pen which you are constantly inscribing in your deeper mind called the book of life. This is why you are making laws, rules and regulations for yourself. Knowing this law, you will proceed to write in your mind thoughts of success, happiness, peace, harmony, abundance, right action and security, thereby leading to a full and happy life.

HOW A SALESMAN GOT RID OF HIS "JINX"

A salesman complained to me that he had failed to make a single sale for four consecutive days and that he was sure that some evil star or bugaboo was against him, because every time he called on a customer, the latter said, "Nothing today," or "Can't see you today."

This salesman became angry and mad at himself, saying to himself, "I'm losing my grip; the cards are stacked against me; I'm a failure." These statements charged with fear lodged in his subconscious mind. The latter, an impersonal law, responded with an automatic movement confirming his inner fears and beliefs in the outer world of affairs. In other words, he decreed a mechanical response from his subconscious mind toward defeatism and failure accompanied with self-criticism and self-condemnation.

How he found the victory within himself

The advice I gave him was that the first step in the restoration of success and good fortune was to cease completely all self-criticism and to look for the God-Presence within him and to choose Divine guidance, right action, harmony and abundance. I explained to him that he possessed the capacity to idealize and imagine consistently success, achievement and victory; if he utilized this ability his deeper mind would then respond accordingly. He began to understand more clearly that his thought and imagery could change his condition, experience and sensations.

This salesman reversed the tide running against him by understanding and applying the following prayer: "From this moment forward, I expect only the best, and I know that invariably the best will come to me. I know good fortune comes to me in multitudinous ways. Whenever I feel prone to condemn or demean myself, I will immediately affirm, 'I exalt God in the midst of me Who is guiding and watching over me in all my ways.' I know my real nature is Divine and that God indwells me and is prospering me in all my ways. I decree success, abundance and accomplishment. Divine love goes before me in all my ways and I am prospering beyond my fondest dreams."

This salesman reconditioned his mind by reiterating the above truths frequently, and he returned to his old stride with a greater ability to give service and increase his sales and his good fortune.

THE PATHETIC CASE OF A FEARFUL MEDICAL STUDENT

Here is part of a letter I received from a medical student. He writes: "I am about to blow my top. I hate one of my professors. I am full of fear that he will fail me and I will be disgraced with my parents. I despise myself. I am morbid and introspective. I am afraid I will explode at the professor and then I'm finished. I'm beside myself with fear."

I asked him to come to see me, since a personal consultation is always more fruitful than a long dissertation by letter. In talking with him, I discovered that this young medical student felt that he should fail. His fear revealed to me that unconsciously he felt inwardly that he should be punished and that the professor should fail him because he was just no good. He admitted that all of this was true. Actually, he was projecting his fear and self-condemnation onto the professor, his parents, and even the university while at the same time, deep down in his heart, he was saying to himself, "I should fail."

The basic reason
for his frustration

Why did this young man want to be a doctor and at the same time, deep within himself, also want to fail his exam? He was brought up in a home where his father was tyrannical and despotic. There was a constant battle between his father and mother. His father set standards much too high for him scholastically and otherwise, and the boy, who could not meet his father's standards, felt he was no good and a failure. As a young boy he despised himself and felt "rejected." Self-pity and self-punishment were his dominant attitudes as a boy, and as an adult *he continually repeated* this sense of rejection and self-denial. When one of the professors was critical of his work, he would go back in his mind to his old hurts and the psychic traumas or hurt thoughts of youth, feeling that he was no good and should be punished; therefore, he was out to hurt himself and destroy four years of medical study.

After gaining an insight into himself and realizing that often we project our fears, animosities and self-condemnation outwardly onto people, environment and invisible forces, he suddenly awakened to the dire results of saying, "I am no good; I'm a failure; I should be punished; I'm a flop; I should jump in the lake." All of these negatives, he realized, were commands to his subconscious mind, which reacted correspondingly. By saying he was no good, his subconscious would see to it that he was no good in his examination, in his relations with people, in his studies and in his contact with the world in general. In addition, he would possibly attract accidents, losses and failure along all lines.

The cure that liberates

Being medically trained, upon reflection he perceived immediately the cause of his condition, and he began to affirm boldly, "The presence of God is my true nature. This presence is all bliss, all harmony, all joy, indivisible, perfect, whole, timeless, ageless and omnipotent. This is my real self which is always the same—

yesterday, today and forever. This is the *I am* within me—the life principle, the supreme and sovereign power, creator of all things visible and invisible.

"The other self of me—my personality—is based on my early training, indoctrination and conditioning, such as the thinking and beliefs of my parents, relatives, teachers and others, who implanted fears, superstitions and other false beliefs in my mind when I was too young to reject them. I can change this personality of mine. I am doing it right now and will continue to give my subconscious mind life-giving patterns of thought and imagery by affirming:

" 'God's love fills my subconscious obliterating all negative patterns of fear. God's river of peace floods my mind. I am full of faith and confidence in the goodness of God, and I know God is guiding me in all ways and Divine right action governs me. I radiate love and goodwill to my professors and all those around me. As I align myself with the Infinite ocean of love, power and beauty, I know I am cleansed and made whole. God loves me and cares for me, and as I draw nigh unto Him He draws nigh unto me.' "

This young medical student went back to college a new and transformed man and wrote me a lovely letter, saying, "I know the meaning now of 'The light dispels the darkness,' and I also know what happens to the crossword puzzle when the answer is known. I use the prayer regularly. I am a new man."

This fledgling doctor could have added what happens to the poison pockets of the subconscious of self-pity, self-denial and self-punishment when you let in the Infinite ocean of love, light, truth and beauty into the polluted stream of the mind. It is cleansed and made whole.

He discovered two natures within himself—the natural man (the five-sense man), usually conditioned by heredity, environment and false theological beliefs, and the spiritual man, which means the presence of God called *I am* in the Bible, which means pure being, the life principle. He exalted the spiritual powers within him and aligned mentally with them, causing these Divine forces to govern his thoughts, feelings, beliefs, actions and reactions. Then the old personality died and the new man in God was born.

Your thoughts come in pairs. The aggressive thoughts of the five-sense or material man must be destroyed, and the thought of God must be resurrected and live in you. *And I, if I be lifted up from the earth, will draw all men unto me* (John 12:32).

POINTS TO RECALL IN THIS CHAPTER

1. Everything comes in pairs. You are conscious, for example, of night and day, ebb and flow, north and south, male and female, positive and negative, in and out, sweet and sour, rest and motion, sickness and health, and sadness and gladness.

2. These opposites in life are halves of the One Whole, which is God in manifestation. These opposites, contrasts and comparisons give us the sensations of being alive.

3. The absolute state is a sense of oneness and wholeness, but when God created the universe, He created the opposites so that we might experience sensations of function and thereby enter into the joy of living and of discovering our true Divinity. God becomes man for the joy of discovering Himself, as there is only God. Every man is God in manifestation.

4. A young boy was determined to go to Australia, but he feared that his mother would not allow the journey. The boy gave attention to the thought of the journey and starved the thought of fear to death by ignoring it and trusting God, and he got his trip.

5. A young woman had an intense desire to marry, but her fear warred with her desire and, as a result, she was frustrated. She feared to repeat the error of a former marriage. She detached her mind from the fear thought and contemplated the qualities she admired in a husband trusting the God-Wisdom to bring it to pass.

6. You enact laws for yourself by your habitual thinking plus the opinions and conceptions you accept as true. Whatever you impress on your subconscious is made manifest as experience, condition and event. With the pen of your thoughts, you can inscribe on your subconscious mind success, guidance, right action, harmony, abundance and security.

7. The so-called "jinx" following the salesman was his self-condemnation, self-criticism and self-loathing. He reversed his mental attitude and joined forces with God within him, affirming boldly that Infinite Intelligence was guiding, directing and advancing him along all lines.

8. A medical student feared he would fail in his final examination, hated one of the professors, and lived in constant fear of abusing or saying something dreadful to the professor. He suddenly realized that his fear was due to the fact that inwardly and unconsciously he felt he should fail, as he felt unworthy and wanted to be punished. He expelled his fear, and thus he became a transformed man.

9. Your thoughts come in pairs. The thoughts of the five-sense man must die, and the thoughts of the indwelling God must be resurrected and live in you.

TWELVE

How Infinite Power
Can Recharge Your Mental
and Spiritual Batteries

Some time ago I had a conversation with a businessman, who finally said to me, "How can I get a quiet mind in a troubled and confused world? I know that it is said 'A quiet mind gets things done.' I'm confused and troubled, and the propaganda in the newspapers, radio and television is driving me half-crazy."

I said to him that I would attempt to throw some light on his problem; provide him with spiritual medicine, which would allay his fears and anxieties; and give him the quiet mind which gets things done. I pointed out that if his thoughts morning, noon and night revolved about war, crime, sickness, disease, accidents and misfortune, he would automatically bring on the mood of depression, anxiety and fear. But if, on the other hand, he gave some of his time and attention to the eternal laws and principles which govern the cosmos and all life, he would automatically be lifted up into the mental atmosphere of inner security and serenity.

HIS SPIRITUAL MEDICINE

As a result, three times a day this man filled his mind with the following truths: *"The heavens declare the glory of God; and the firmament sheweth his handiwork* (Ps. 19:1) . I know a Supreme Intelligence governs the planets in their courses and controls and directs the entire universe. I know there is Divine law and order

121

operating with absolute certainty fashioning the entire world, causing the stars to come nightly to the sky, and regulating the galaxies in space; and God is ruling the universe. I move mentally into the stillness of my own mind and contemplate these eternal truths of God.

"Thou wilt keep him in perfect peace, whose mind is stayed on thee: because he trusteth in thee (Isa. 26:3) .

Peace I leave with you, my peace I give unto you: not as the world giveth, give I unto you. Let not your heart be troubled, neither let it be afraid (John 14:27) .

"For God is not the author of confusion, but of peace . . . (I Cor. 14:33) .

"And let the peace of God rule in your heart . . . (Col. 3:15) ."

FOCUSING ON THE BIG THINGS OF LIFE

This businessman turned away from the concerns and worries of the day and gave attention to the great principles and truths of life, contemplated them, and focused his attention on them. He forgot the little things and began to think about the great, the wonderful and the good. When he turned away from the trials and troubles of the world and refused to describe them or even talk about them at any length, his anxiety and worry diminished and he developed a quiet mind in a troubled world. He decided to let the peace of God rule in his heart. Consequently, his business ran smoother under much better decisions which he could now make.

HOW A HARASSED MOTHER CONQUERED HER "HEART TROUBLE" AND AGGRAVATIONS

A young housewife suffered from insomnia and from continuous heart palpitation. She felt certain that she had a cardiac condition. She was depressed and constantly giving vent to anger, impatience and hostility toward her husband and children. The headlines in the newspaper annoyed her terribly, and she wrote vitriolic and critical letters to her congressman. I sent her to a heart specialist. He said there was nothing organically wrong with her, but that she was full of emotional conflicts and mad at the world.

I explained to her that her anger and emotional turmoil toward her family and others would be dissolved when she began to pursue a pattern of prayer, and that as she tuned in on the Infinite Presence and Power she would discover that she would be suffused and saturated with the order, harmony, love and calmness which she would touch in her period of quiet contemplation of things Divine. I explained further that she could then expect an automatic response from her deeper mind making her poised, serene and calm; in addition, she would have the feeling of goodwill to all. I emphasized that she was to cease completely talking about her ailments and her worries and anxieties about world conditions, for that would only magnify her inner troubles and make her condition worse, because her mind always amplifies what it looks upon.

A technique for
inner poise and calm

She concentrated on the following healing verses of the Bible knowing that as she did so, these truths would penetrate into her subconscious and make her radiant, happy, joyous and free. These are the verses which I wrote out for her:

Have not I commanded thee? Be strong and of a good courage; be not afraid, neither be thou dismayed: for the Lord thy God is with thee whithersoever thou goest (Josh. 1:9).

And we know that all things work together for good to them that love God . . . (Rom. 8:28).

Casting all your care upon Him; for He careth for you (I Pet. 5:7).

The Lord is my shepherd; I shall not want. He maketh me to lie down in green pastures: he leadeth me beside the still waters. Thou preparest a table before me in the presence of mine enemies: thou anointest my head with oil; my cup runneth over. Surely goodness and mercy shall follow me all the days of my life: and I will dwell in the house of the Lord for ever (Ps. 23: 1, 2, 5, 6).

Focusing her attention on this spiritual food, she quickly found the peace that passeth understanding.

HOW TO MAINTAIN A SERENE MIND

In talking to many business and professional men of different religious persuasions, they have informed me that regularly and periodically they go to a church retreat where they listen to talks on God, prayer and the art of meditation, and then they enter into a silent period. After a morning meditation, they are told to contemplate what they heard and remain silent for several days, even during mealtime. All this time they are requested to dwell calmly and quietly on the instructions and meditations given each morning.

All of them have told me that they come back renewed, refreshed and replenished spiritually and mentally. Following their return to their offices, factories and professional lives, they continue to maintain quiet periods for fifteen to twenty minutes every day, morning and evening, and they have found that what the Bible says is true: *The peace of God, which passeth all understanding, shall keep your hearts and minds . . .* (Phil. 4:7).

Benefits of recharging mental and spiritual batteries

Having spiritually recharged their mental and spiritual batteries, these men are able to meet head on and, with faith, courage and confidence, cope with the problems, strife, vexations and contentions of the day. These men know where to receive renewed spiritual power—by tuning in quietly, as Emerson says, with the Infinite, which lies stretched in smiling repose. Energy, power, inspiration, guidance and wisdom come out of the silence and the stillness of the mind when tuned in with God. These men have learned to relax and to give up their egoistic pride. They have recognized, honored and called upon a wisdom and power that created all things visible and invisible and that governs all things ceaselessly, timelessly and forever. They have decided to go the way of wisdom. *Her ways are ways of pleasantness, and all her paths are peace* (Prov. 3:17).

THE QUIET MIND IS WITHIN YOUR REACH

If I offer you a gift of a book, in order to receive it, you must reach for it by stretching forth your hand. In like manner, since all the riches of God are within you, you must make some effort to claim them. God is the giver and the gift, but you are the receiver. Open your mind and heart and let in God's river of peace. Let it fill your mind and heart, for God is peace.

Contemplate the following verses of the Eighth Psalm and you will find a deep river of life, love, quiescence and equanimity steal over the barren areas of your mind bringing rest to the troubled soul:

When I consider thy heavens, the work of thy fingers, the moon and the stars, which thou hast ordained; What is man, that thou art mindful of him? and the son of man, that thou visitest him? For thou hast made him a little lower than the angels, and hast crowned him with glory and honour. Thou madest him to have dominion over the works of thy hands; thou hast put all things under his feet (Ps. 8:3, 4, 5, 6).

Meditating on the eternal verities contained in this Psalm and on the immeasurable nature of the universe to which we belong, the Infinite Mind and Infinite Intelligence, which created us and which animates and supports us, and which moves rhythmically, harmoniously, ceaselessly, changelessly and with mathematical precision, gives you faith, confidence, strength and security. Know that you have, as the Psalmist says, dominion over your thoughts, feelings, actions and reactions in life. This fills you with self-esteem and a sense of worthiness and power, which endows you with strength to do your work, live joyously, and walk the earth with the praise of God forever on your lips.

HOW INNER CONFLICT CAN BE CALMED

One day in Beverly Hills, a man who recognized me stopped me on the street and said that he was terribly disturbed. He asked, "Do you think I can get a quiet mind? I have been at war with myself for over two months." There was a conflict raging within him. He was full of fears, doubts, hates and religious bigotry. He was furious because his daughter had married into a different faith, and he said that he hated her husband. He was not on speaking terms with his own son because the son joined the armed forces and he (the father) belonged to a peace crusade. And to top things off, his wife was suing him for divorce.

I was not able to give him much time on the street corner, but I told him briefly that he should be delighted that his daughter had married the man of her dreams and that, if they loved each other, they certainly should marry, as love knows no creed, race, dogma or color. Love is God, and God is impersonal and no respecter of persons. Regarding his son, I suggested that he write the young man and tell him how much he loves him and to pray for him. I said he should respect his son's decision and not interfere with him other than to wish for him all the blessings of life. I also told him that I gathered from his conversation that the bickering and quarreling in their marriage was probably due to an unresolved childhood conflict with his mother and that he expected his wife to be a substitute for his mother.

I wrote down on a piece of paper these everlasting truths and gave them to him to read and digest: "Thou wilt keep him in perfect peace, whose mind is stayed on Thee, because he trusteth in Thee." I urged him to keep his mind focused on God with trust, faith and certainty, and that he would then feel the river of life, love and inner quietude filling his heart. I added that whenever he thought of anyone in his family, he was to say, "God's peace fills my soul and God's peace fills his or her soul."

How this healing
was accomplished

A few days later I had a note from this man, which said, "Life was like hell for me. I hated to open my eyes in the morning. I took phenobarbitol every night in order to sleep. After I left you on the street, though, I surrendered my family and myself to God and affirmed constantly: 'God will keep me in perfect peace, because my mind is stayed on Him.' The change that has come over me is unbelievable. Life has become full of joy and wonder.

My wife cancelled divorce proceedings and we are back together again. I wrote letters to my daughter and son-in-law and to my son, and there are peace, harmony and understanding among us all."

All that this man did was get all the hatred and resentment out of his heart. As he surrendered to the golden river of peace within, it flowed in response to him, and all the pieces fell into place in Divine order.

HOW A "VICTIM OF CIRCUMSTANCES" STOPPED BEING A VICTIM

During the summer months I had the pleasure of conducting a seminar near Denver, Colorado. While there I interviewed a man who said, "I'm fenced in, frustrated, unhappy and blocked at every turn of the road. I want to sell my ranch and get away, but I feel like I'm in jail—just stuck."

"Well," I said, "if I hypnotized you now, you would believe yourself to be whatever I suggested you were, because your conscious mind, which reasons and judges and weighs, would be suspended and your subconscious mind, being noncontroversial, would accept whatever suggestion is given to it. If I suggested to you that you were an Indian guide and you were to track down a criminal, you would proceed stealthily to look for him in the mountains.

"If I told you you were in jail and said you can get out, you would feel yourself a prisoner and you would believe yourself in jail surrounded by walls and bars of steel. Following my suggestion, you would make frenetic efforts to escape. You would try to jump over the walls; you would look for the keys and try to break out; and you would go through all the efforts to escape. All the time you are here in the wide open spaces of Colorado as free as the wind. All this is due to the amenability of your subconscious to its suggestions, which it faithfully executes.

"Likewise, you have suggested to your subconscious mind that you can't sell the ranch, that you are a prisoner here, that you can't go to Denver and do what you want to do, that you are in debt, and that you are blocked at every turn. Your subconscious mind has no alternative but to accept the suggestions you give it, as it is oblivious to everything but that which you impress upon it.

Actually, you have mesmerized and hypnotized yourself. Your bondage and restrictions are self-imposed, and you are suffering and in continuous mental conflict from your false opinions and beliefs."

Learning how to think rightly

I suggested he follow age-old truths: "Be ye transformed by the renewing of your mind. Repent, for the Kingdom of Heaven is at hand." *To repent* means to think again—to think from the standpoint of basic principles and eternal verities. I told him to stand up boldly and claim his good, for, as Shakespeare said, "All things be ready if the mind be so." I added that he had to ready and prepare his mind to receive his good now, for the kingdom of harmony, health, peace, guidance, abundance and security is at hand, waiting only for him to accept and take his good now.

The "prescription" which rescued him

"My mind is now absorbed, interested and fascinated in the eternal, changeless truths of God. I now still my mind and contemplate the great truth that God indwells me and walks and talks in me. I still the wheels of my mind and know that God indwells me. I know this and believe it. 'It is the Father's good pleasure to give me to the kingdom.' 'Commit thy way unto the Lord: trust also in Him; and he shall bring it to pass.'

"Infinite Intelligence draws the buyer who wants my ranch, he prospers in it, there is a Divine exchange, and we are both blessed. The buyer is right and the price is right, and the deeper currents of my subconscious mind bring both of us together in Divine order. I know that 'all things be ready if the mind be so.' When worry thoughts come to my mind, I will immediately affirm, 'None of these things move me.' I know I am reconditioning my mind to stillness, relaxation, equanimity and imperturbability. I am making a new world of freedom, abundance and security for myself."

A few weeks later I had a telephone call from this rancher telling me that he had sold his ranch and was thus free to go to

Denver. He was no longer a prisoner of his mind. He said, "I realized I put myself in a prison of want, limitation and restriction by my negative thinking and that, actually, I was self-hypnotized."

This man learned that his thought was creative and that all his frustration was due to the suggestions of others, which he accepted, although he could have rejected them, and that events, circumstances and conditions were not causative. They suggested fears and limitations which he indulged instead of completely rejecting them, realizing that straight-line thinking was the only cause and power in his world. His repeated meditation gave him power to think constructively and proved to him his capacity to choose wisely from universal principles.

When anxieties, worries and fears come to you, maintain your inner equilibrium and affirm, "I will lift up mine eyes to the hills from whence cometh my strength," and firmly announce to yourself also, *None of these things move me* (Acts 20:24).

POINTS TO RECALL IN THIS CHAPTER

1. If you begin thinking morning, noon and night about all the calamities in the world—the crimes, disasters, sickness and tragedies—you will mentally drag yourself down in a miasma of morbid thinking and consequently bring on yourself depression and melancholia. Realize that Divine law and order govern the world and you will be lifted up and enter into the world of reverence for things Divine.

2. Mentally retreat into the stillness of your mind and contemplate the undeviating laws and principles behind all things. Keep your mind on God and you will possess the serene mind and accomplish the attainments of your desires.

3. Refuse to describe your symptoms, troubles and worries, and they will grow less. Think big and tune in with God.

4. Anger, emotional turmoil and animosity toward others will be dissolved as you practice the art of effective prayer, which is contemplating the truths of God from the highest standpoint.

5. You still the discordant wheels of your mind when you slowly repeat the 23rd Psalm to yourself. Then quietly contemplate for fifteen or twenty minutes the meaning of these

verses to you. You will then meet triumphantly all the challenges of the day.

6. Cosmic Good is the giver and the gift. You are the receiver. Reach out mentally now to accept God's river of peace and let it flood your mind and heart. God is peace, and His peace awaits your acceptance, for God is the eternal now. Why wait for it, take it NOW.

7. A marvelous psalm to instill in your mind for balance, confidence, dignity and a deep reverence for things Divine is the Eighth Psalm. It is a marvelous spiritual prescription for fruitful serenity.

8. When two people of different religious beliefs love each other, love transcends all religious and institutionalized dogma, and they should marry.

9. You are not a victim of circumstances, conditions, heredity or environment. Think from the standpoint of principle, and the creative law of your mind will respond according to the nature of your thought.

THIRTEEN

How to Use the Infinite Power to Guide You in All Ways

There is a principle of Divine Guidance operating in you and throughout the universe, and by using the Infinite Intelligence within you, you can attract many wonderful experiences and happenings beyond your fondest dreams. This chapter will reveal to you the principles of guidance in a variety of ways, so that you may apply them to attract all kinds of blessings into your life.

HOW A WOMAN ATTRACTED HER RIGHT MATE

A young secretary who had made two previous mistakes in marriage said to me, "I don't want to make a third mistake. I know the last two errors were made because I judged according to appearance, and I don't know how to apply the principle of guidance in my life. Check and see if my present prayer is correct." The following was her prayer:

"Infinite Intelligence within me attracts to me my right spouse. He is harmonious, most likeable, friendly, and spiritual minded. I contribute to his joy and happiness and there are harmony, peace, and understanding between us. I believe definitely that Infinite Intelligence responds to my thought, and I know It makes no mistake. I expect and I definitely and positively believe I will meet my right mate. I know the principle is now working and I walk the earth in the light that it is so."

131

I commended her on her written prayer and the intelligence and wisdom shown in the application of the powers within her. The principle of Divine Guidance went to work for her, and she attracted an interesting, enjoyable, and wonderful man. I subsequently had the privilege of conducting their marriage ceremony.

HOW DIVINE GUIDANCE WORKS FOR ANOTHER

You can use the Infinite Power to guide someone other than yourself, whether the other be a stranger, relative, or close friend. You can do this by knowing that the Infinite Guiding Power is responsive to your thought and by believing in this Infinite response. I have done this for many people with extraordinary and fascinating results.

For example, a young engineer called me on the phone one day and said, "The organization I am with is selling out to a larger firm, and I am told I am not needed in the new setup. Would you pray for Divine Guidance for me?" I told him that there was an Infinite Guiding Principle which would reveal a new door of expression for him, and all that he had to do was to believe that this is so in the same way that he believed in Boyle's Law or Avogadro's Law in science.

I used the principle as follows: I pictured this engineer saying to me, "I found a wonderful position with a wonderful salary. It came to me 'out of the blue.'" I did this for about three or four minutes after he hung up the phone and then forgot all about it. I believed and expected an answer.

The following day he called me and confirmed the fact that he had accepted a good offer with a new engineering firm. The offer, he said, came to him "out of the blue"!

There is but one Mind, and what I subjectively pictured and felt as true came to pass in the experience of the engineer. When you call upon the Infinite Guiding Principle, It always answers you. What you believe will take place will surely happen.

HOW TO RECEIVE PERSONAL GUIDANCE
FOR TRUE PLACE

You build up confidence and trust in the Infinite Guiding Force by knowing that God is Infinite Life and that you are eternal life made manifest. The Life Principle is interested in seeking expression through you. You are unique and entirely different. You think, speak, and act differently. There is no one in all the world like you. The Life Principle never repeats Itself. Realize, know, and believe that you have special and unique talents and capabilities. You can do something in a special way that no one else in all the world can do because you are you. You are here to express yourself fully and to do what you love to do, thereby fulfilling your destiny in life. You are important. You are an organ or expression of God. God hath need of you where you are; otherwise, you would not be here. The Presence of God indwells you. All the powers, attributes, and qualities of God are within you. You have faith, imagination, and the power to choose and think. You mold, fashion, and create your own destiny by the way you think.

HOW THE GUIDING PRINCIPLE SAVED A LIFE

The late Dr. Harry Gaze, author of *Emmet Fox, The Man and His Work,* believed in the Principle of Guidance in all his undertakings. One time he was about to board a plane, and an inner voice told him not to go. His bags were on the plane already, but he had them taken off and cancelled the trip. He followed this intuitive impulse, and it saved his life because all those on that particular plane were lost.

His favorite Bible passage was, *He shall give his angels charge over thee, to keep thee in all thy ways. They shall bear thee up in their hands, lest thou dash thy foot against a stone* (Ps. 91:11, 12).

RIGHT ACTION IS FOR YOU THROUGH GUIDANCE

Divine Guidance comes when your motives are right, and when your real inner desire is to do the right thing. When your thought is right, i.e., when it conforms to the Golden Rule and the law of goodwill for all, a feeling of inner peace and tranquility wells up within you. This inner feeling of poise, balance, and equanimity causes you to do the right thing in all phases of your life. When you sincerely wish for others what you wish for yourself, then you are practicing love, which is the fulfillment of the law of health, happiness, and peace of mind.

How you can be
guided automatically

A friend of mine, a builder, is always busy and can't adequately handle all his business calls. He said to me, "They tell me the building business is slow, but I can't keep up with the calls on me." He added that he had made lots of mistakes in the past and had lost two small fortunes in bad ventures, but six years ago he sat down, studied *The Power of Your Subconscious Mind,*[1] and immediately began to apply the principles described therein. He showed me his daily prayer typed neatly on a card, which he carries with him all the time. It read as follows: "I forgive myself for all the mistakes of the past. I blame no one. All my mistakes were stepping-stones to my success, prosperity, and advancement. I believe implicitly that God is guiding me always and that whatever I do will be right. I go forward confidently without fear. I give the best that is in me to all my work. I feel, believe, claim and know that I am lifted up, guided, directed, sustained, prospered, and protected in all ways. I do the right thing, I think the right thoughts, and I know there is an Infinite Intelligence in my subconscious mind that answers me. I give the best to my customers. I am guided to give the right price, and I am inspired to see what is to be done and I do it. I attract the right men, who work harmoniously with me. I know these thoughts sink into my subconscious mind forming a subjective pattern, and I believe I will get an automatic response from my subconscious mind in accordance with my habitual thinking."

This is the builder's daily prayer, and he is automatically guided to all good. He said to me that everything he does seems to have the touch of Midas, the Golden Touch for prosperity. There have been no errors, losses, or labor disputes in his ranks in over six years. Truly, he is automatically guided, as you can be too.

Remember, your subconscious mind responds to the nature of your conscious mind's thinking and imagery.

HOW DIVINE GUIDANCE REVEALED TRUE TALENTS

A young man who had failed in the musical field, in the theatre as an actor, and in business also, said to me, "I have failed in

---

[1] Joseph Murphy, *The Power of Your Subconscious Mind* (Englewood Cliffs, N.J.: Prentice-Hall, Inc., 1963).

everything." I suggested to him that the answer to his problem was within himself and that he could find out his true expression in life. I explained to him that when he was doing what he loved to do, he would be happy, successful, and prosperous.

At my suggestion, he prayed as follows: "I have the power to rise higher in life. I have now come to a clear-cut decision that I was born to succeed and lead a triumphant, constructive life. I have reached the inner conviction that the royal road to success is mine now. Infinite Intelligence within me reveals my hidden talents, and I follow the lead which comes into my conscious, reasoning mind. I recognize it clearly. Success is mine now. Wealth is mine. I am doing what I love to do, and I am serving humanity in a wonderful way. I believe in the Principle of Guidance, and I know the answer comes, as it is done unto me as I believe."

After a few weeks, this young man had an intense desire to study for the ministry along the lines of the Science of the Mind. Today he is a tremendous success as a teacher, minister, and counselor, and he is immensely happy in his work. He discovered an Infinite Guiding Principle that knew his inner talents and which revealed them to him according to his belief.

HOW A FORTUNE IN MIND WAS DISCOVERED BY AN 80-YEAR-OLD WOMAN

I had a most interesting conversation with a woman over eighty years of age who is alert, mentally alive, illumined, inspired, and quickened by the Divine Spirit, which animates her entire being. She told me that for several weeks she had asked her Higher Self prior to sleep, "My Higher Self reveals to me a new idea, which is complete in my mind and which I can visualize with the greatest facility. This idea blesses all people." She was given the model of a new invention complete in her mind. She in turn gave the drawing to her son, who is an engineer, and he submitted it to a patent attorney, who had it patented. She has been offered $50,000 by one organization for the patent, plus a percentage of the sales.

She believed that the Supreme Intelligence within her, the Infinite Guiding Principle, would respond, and that the idea would be complete, including every possible improvement needed. Her prayer was answered just as she had expected, visualized, and planned.

Regardless of your profession, business, trade, or occupation, you have the power to still your mind and call upon the Infinite Intelligence of your subconscious to reveal to you a new idea that will bless you and the world. You can firmly believe that you will secure an answer. *Before they call, I will answer; and while they are yet speaking, I will hear* (Isa. 65:24). The answer to all things is already within you. It was there from the foundation of time. God indwells you and God knows the answer.

HOW THE GUIDING PRINCIPLE ATTRACTS WHAT YOU LOOK FOR

A friend of mine wrote me from Ireland saying that a farm belonging to an uncle had been bequeathed to her brother, who had gone to America in 1922, and from whom they had never heard. She asked if it would be possible to find him and write to him. They had hired an attorney in Ireland, but he could find nothing and had received not the slightest clue. My friend did not even have a picture of her brother.

I sat down one night, quieted my mind, and read the 23rd Psalm, which is the most wonderful Psalm for rest, repose, and quietude. In this Psalm we are told that David revealed that the Lord guided him and led him to green pastures and still waters, which means that the Infinite Guiding Principle reveals answers to man and guides him to peaceful, happy, and joyous situations. David believed in this Guiding Principle, and It responded to his belief in It. The Lord he referred to is the Creative Intelligence resident in one's subconscious mind[2] which created you and sustains you.

Meditating on the wisdom of this Psalm, I mused one evening as follows: "The Infinite Guiding Principle which guides the planets in their courses and causes the sun to shine and governs the entire cosmos is the same Guiding Principle in me. It knows all and sees all. This Supreme Intelligence knows where this man is and reveals the answer. He communicates with his sister at once. There is but one mind, and there is no separation in the Mind-Principle. Furthermore, there is no time or space in mind. I decree now that his whereabouts is immediately known and revealed to his sister

---

2 Joseph Murphy, *The Power of Your Subconscious Mind* (Englewood Cliffs, N.J.: Prentice-Hall, Inc., 1963).

and her attorney in Ireland. This Infinite Intelligence within me knows best how to do this and takes care of it in Its own way. I believe this, I accept it, and I give thanks it is done now."

The way the Guiding Principle worked is most revealing and inspiring. A few weeks had transpired, when I received an air mail letter from my friend in Ireland, in which she said that her brother had sent her a cablegram saying he was on his way home for a visit. This was the first word she had heard from him since April, 1922, a lapse of forty-six years. This was not a coincidence or pure chance. This is a universe of law and order. Nothing happens by chance. As Emerson says, "Everything is pushed from behind." There is a law of cause and effect which is cosmic and universal. My thought entered into the universal subconscious mind, in which we all live, move, and have our being, and which permeates the entire cosmos. This was picked up by the missing brother, and the Guiding Principle of Life compelled him to communicate immediately with his sister.

A subsequent letter from my friend stated that her brother told her that one night he could not sleep, as there was a persistent, nagging, unrelenting urge to visit his old home and call his sister. He responded immediately to the psychic urge by sending her a cable and arranging for air passage to Ireland. On arrival at his old home, he found that the promptings and whisperings of his deeper mind had proved to be a blessing, since he not only inherited a wonderful farm but also a lovely home.

You cannot determine how the answer to your prayer will come. The Bible says, *For as the heavens are higher than the earth, so are my ways higher than your ways, and my thoughts than your thoughts* (Isa. 55:9).

POINTS TO RECALL IN THIS CHAPTER

1. You can learn from your mistakes. Realize they are stepping-stones to your success. There is a Cosmic Guiding Principle that responds to your belief in It.

2. You can use the Guiding Principle to guide and direct another person by realizing there is only one mind, and that the same Infinite Intelligence which guides the planets in their courses will guide, direct, and reveal the right

answer to the other person. Your belief will be communicated instantaneously to the person you are praying for, and he or she will experience the joy of the answered prayer. What you believe will take place and will surely happen.

3. You can discover your hidden talents and true expression in life by calling on the Guiding Principle within you and affirming with conviction, "Infinite Intelligence reveals my hidden talents to me and opens up the perfect way for the highest expression of my talents. I follow the lead which comes into my conscious, reasoning mind."

4. The Guiding Principle can protect you from harm and warn you of impending danger. The late Dr. Harry Gaze regularly dwelt on two verses of the 91st Psalm (verses 11 and 12), and Divine protection was given him, which saved his life.

5. Divine right action comes to you when your motives are right and when you really desire to do the right thing, in conformity with the Golden Rule and the law of love.

6. Many people experience automatic guidance because they have convinced their subconscious minds that they believe they will always be guided to do the right thing, and their subconscious responds accordingly. Feel, believe, claim, and know that you are guided, directed, sustained, and blessed at all times. As you continue to reiterate these truths, you will be automatically guided.

7. Come to a clear-cut decision that you were born to succeed and to lead a triumphant and constructive life. Claim and believe the royal road to success is yours now, and the Cosmic Guiding Principle will guide you to victory, triumph, and phenomenal success.

8. You can discover that there is a fortune in your mind. Call upon Infinite Intelligence within you to reveal a new creative idea which will bless you and humanity. Affirm that the idea is complete in your mind and that you visualize it clearly. The answer will come. All you must do is believe. According to your belief is it done unto you.

9. If you are looking for a long lost friend or relative, and you don't know where the person is, realize Cosmic Intelligence knows all and sees all. Affirm boldly, knowing and believing the answer will come, "Cosmic Intelligence

knows where John is and reveals his whereabouts in Divine order. I release this to the ocean of my subjective mind, and it reveals the answer in its own way." As you meditate this way, you will experience the joy of the answered prayer. *In all thy ways acknowledge Him, and He shall direct thy paths* (Prov. 3:6) .

FOURTEEN

How to Use the Infinite Power to Heal

The Cosmic Healing Power which made your body also knows how to heal it. There is an Infinite Healing Presence within you that knows all the processes and functions of your body. When you "tune in" with this Infinite Power, It will become active and potent in your life. The Bible says, *I am the Lord that healeth thee* (Exod. 15:26).

It is your Divine birthright to be healthy, vital, strong and dynamic. This chapter will point out vividly what processes and steps you can take to induce and experience radiant health. I suggest you begin to practice the methods and techniques outlined in this chapter, because you will thereby find the way to health, harmony, and serenity.

GOOD HEALTH IS SECURED THROUGH CONSTRUCTIVE THINKING

The Book of Proverbs says, *For as he thinketh in his heart, so is he* (Prov. 23:7). The heart means your subconscious mind. The thoughts, opinions, and beliefs implanted in your subconscious mind are made manifest in your body, in your business, and in all your other affairs. Your health is controlled very largely by the way you think all day long. By guiding your mind toward thoughts of wholeness, beauty, perfection and vitality, you will experience a sense of well-being. If you dwell on thoughts of worry, fear, hate, jealousy, depression, and sorrow, you will experience sickness of mind, body, and affairs. You are what you think all day long.

HOW THE INFINITE HEALING POWER
CAN BE RELEASED

I sent a young woman suffering from a chronic sore throat and a persistent fever to a physician friend of mine. He diagnosed it as a "strep" throat and gave her antibiotics and a solution to gargle. However, she did not respond to the antibiotics and antifebric medication. He could not find any reason why she didn't respond to the treatment. She came back to see me at my request. I asked her if she were holding something back from me; and, if so, if she talked it out with me, possibly a healing would follow.

She blurted out, "I hate my mother and where I live. She is domineering and demanding, and wants to control my life by making me marry a man whom she thinks is right for me."

This emotional state of resentment plus a guilt feeling for hating her mother caused the flare-up in her throat accompanied by a fever. I explained to her that her ambivalent state of love and hate, in which at one moment she said that she loved her mother and the next moment that she hated her, was undoubtedly the cause of her unhealthy condition. She did not want to marry the man, so her subconscious mind accommodated her by bringing about inflammation and infection of her throat. Her subconscious was actually saying to her conscious mind, "you can't marry him as long as you are sick." That was her body's manner of agreeing with her subconscious desire.

How her health was
restored to normal

At my suggestion she informed her mother definitely and positively that she was not going to marry the man, as she did not love him. Furthermore, she established her own residence and decided to make all her own decisions. I was able to talk with the mother, and I pointed out to her that it was completely wrong to try to insist that her daughter marry a man whom she did not love, and that marriage for any other reason than love would be a sham, a farce, and a masquerade.

The mother wisely agreed and told her daughter she could marry whomever she wished, that she would no longer tell her what to do, and that she was as free as the wind.

A demonstrated
miracle of healing

This young woman had a heart-to-heart talk with her mother, and both of them entered into the spirit of forgiveness, love, and goodwill for each other. Immediately there was a perfect healing, and she has had no physical trouble since.

HOW TO RELEASE NEW HEALTH-GIVING POWER

Recently I chatted with a young banker who seemed very nervous, jittery, and apparently ill in mind and body. He said, "I've got the Asian bug. This 'flu' is wearing me down." I wrote out a mental and spiritual prescription for him, emphasizing that by repetition, belief, and expectancy the ideas of health, wholeness, and strength would penetrate his subconscious mind, and he would get marvelous results.

A metaphysical
prescription for health

Here is my prescription: "I am strong, powerful, loving, harmonious, vital, dynamic, joyful and happy." He repeated this affirmation for about five minutes three or four times a day, knowing that whatever he attached to "I am" he would become. At the end of about a week, he called me on the phone and said, "That spiritual medicine you gave me worked like a miracle. From now on I will make sure that whatever I attach to 'I am' will be God-like and of good report." He expected results and believed in the response of his subconscious.

THE INFINITE HEALING POWER OF YOUR
SUBCONSCIOUS MIND

A mother brought her ten-year-old boy to see me. This boy had developed a bad case of asthma. The mother said that when the summer came and the boy went to live with his grandparents in San Francisco, he was completely free from attack; but when he came back home, he invariably suffered a relapse and had to resume the medication of his physician, which helped alleviate his distress.

In talking to the boy alone, I learned that his father and mother were always quarreling, that he was afraid he would lose both of them, and that he would no longer have a home. This boy was perfectly normal in every way. The trouble was the contention and strife in the home. During a conference with his mother, I found that she felt a tremendous hostility and suppressed rage toward her husband. She admitted that she occasionally threw dishes at him, and that in two instances he had beaten her up. The boy was caught in this emotional cross-fire and consequently suffered from fear and a deep sense of insecurity.

A miraculous working
of Infinite Healing Power

I succeeded in getting the father and mother together and proceeded to explain to them how children suffer from the mental and emotional climate of the home atmosphere. I said that, undoubtedly, they both loved the boy. I pointed out that inasmuch as they had brought him into the world, they had a moral and spiritual obligation to see to it that there was love, peace, and harmony in the home; moreover, they should convey to the boy that he was loved, wanted, and appreciated. I elaborated on the fact that the boy wanted a feeling of security; and that when love and harmony between his father and mother were restored, I believed the asthmatic condition would go away. His asthma was the symptom of his fear and anxiety.

The healing prayer by father
and mother for their son

I wrote out a prayer for the boy's father and mother and suggested that they alternate with one another praying night and morning, knowing that as they prayed for each other and their son, all the pent up hatred and animosity would be dissolved by Divine love. The following is the prayer: "Both of us join together in knowing that God is and His Infinite Healing Power is flowing through each one of us. We radiate love, peace, and goodwill to each other. We see the presence of God in one another and we speak kindly, lovingly, and harmoniously to one another. We lift each other up mentally and spiritually by knowing the light, love, and joy of God are being expressed more and more every day by each one of us. We salute the Divinity in each other, and our marriage grows more blessed and beautiful every day. Our son is open and receptive to our loving thoughts. He lives, moves, and has his being in God. He breathes the pure breath of Spirit and his bronchial tubes, lungs, and entire respiratory system are permeated and saturated by the vitalizing and harmonizing Infinite Healing Power of his subconscious mind, thus making his breathing free, easy, and perfect." They repeated their prayer three or four times each morning and night, the hubsand in the morning and the wife at night.

Healing prayer for
the son to follow

Here is the prayer the boy followed each night: "I love my father and mother. God loves them and cares for them. They are happy together. I inhale the peace of God and I exhale the love of God. I sleep in peace and I wake in joy."

The father and mother voiced the prayer given them regularly and believed in the miracle working power of their subconscious mind. At the end of about two weeks, they noticed the boy was completely free from the wheezing attacks and discontinued all medication. The boy told me that he had had a dream on the seventh night following his prayer wherein a man with a beard appeared to him and said, "Sonny, you are all right now." He woke up and told his father and mother what had happened and said to them, "I know I am healed."

My analysis and comment

I believe that when the parents began to pray together and for each other, as well as for their son, the healing vibrations of peace, harmony, and love impinged on the receptive mind of the boy, resurrecting the wholeness, harmony, and perfection already resident in his subconscious mind. They believed in the Infinite Healing Power of his subconscious mind, believed in what they were doing, and why they were doing it. Furthermore, the boy's prayer accelerated the healing process. In filling his mind with faith and confidence in the healing power of God and with love for his parents, his subconscious mind dramatized the healing which took place in a vivid dream. The Bible says, *I the Lord will make myself known unto him in a vision, and will speak unto him in a dream* (Num. 12:6).

THE MIRACLE OF CHANGED ATTITUDE CHANGES LIVES

At the close of the nineteenth century, William James, referred to as the father of American psychology, said, "The greatest discovery in my generation is that human beings can alter their lives by altering their attitudes of mind." That is to say, you can have a greater measure of health, vitality, aliveness, and buoyancy if you begin to feed your subconscious mind with life giving patterns of harmony, joy, strength, power, energy, enthusiasm, and victory.

How changed attitude healed a baffling illness

A few weeks ago I spoke to about 1500 people assembled in the ballroom of the Frontier Hotel in Las Vegas, Nevada. I gave a talk on "How to Develop the Healing Consciousness." After the lecture, a young doctor told me of a very interesting and inspiring experience. He said that one night he was called to a home where the parents of a sick girl did not believe in sickness or disease or doctors of any school. The father said to him, "My daughter is charged with fear and is afraid she'll die." The doctor examined the girl and told her that her temperature was 102 degrees, but that she would be all right—there was nothing radically wrong and she was in no danger of death.

She asked him to pray with her, and he being very religious, did so by quietly reciting the 23rd Psalm with her. She would not take any medicine because it was contrary to her religious belief. He told me that he believed she would be all right, and he pictured her as perfect.

A month later, the girl's brother, who had wandered away from the religious beliefs of his parents and sister, and had become in his own right a very successful medical doctor and surgeon, visited the physician and wanted to know what therapy he had given his sister, as she had been suffering from severe epileptic seizures two or three times every week and had now become free from all symptoms and attacks. He said he had tried unsuccessfully to get her to take modern anti-epileptic drugs for several years. The young doctor told the patient's brother that he used no therapy other than suggesting that she would be all right, that there was no danger of death and that she would recover immediately.

They were both flabbergasted and dumbfounded for a few moments. The patient's brother broke the silence by saying, "All I know is that you gave her a transfusion of faith in the healing power of God, and your positive suggestion found its way to her subconscious mind, which healed her."

This young doctor said to me, "Had I known she had epilepsy, I would never have been so positive and confident in my approach to her. I can now see that my image of perfect health and complete confidence in her recovery was communicated to her subconscious mind and that my attitude coupled with her new attitude changed everything and brought forth a perfect healing.

"One year has passed," he said, "and she has not had a single seizure. She is now married and drives her own car." Changed attitudes can change everything for the better!

The Bible says, *Thy faith hath made thee whole; go in peace* (Luke 8:48).

POINTS TO RECALL IN THIS CHAPTER

1. The Cosmic Intelligence made your body, knows all its processes and functions, and knows how to heal you.

2. Your health is what you think all day long. Dwell on thoughts of health, wholeness, vitality, power, strength, and harmony. Busy your mind with these thoughts and your body will reflect your habitual thinking.

3. Negative emotions can cause many diseases. Destructive emotions get snarled up in your subconscious mind, and, being negative, must have a negative outlet in the form of various organic malfunctions.

4. When you come to a clear-cut decision, the mental conflict is dissolved. When you refuse to be dominated by others and decide to run your own life and make all your own decisions and enter into the spirit of forgiveness of others, your particular illness, mental or otherwise, may well disappear.

5. Whatever you attach to "I am" you become. For radiant health, affirm frequently, "I am strong, powerful, radiant, happy, joyous, and vital." Make a habit of this and you will experience miraculous results.

6. The mental and emotional atmosphere of the home affects the health and disposition of the children. Children grow in the image and likeness of the dominant mental climate of the parents. Parents should exalt God in the midst of each other and radiate love, peace, and goodwill to one another. As they pray together for harmony, health, and peace, and as they surround the children with light, love, truth, and beauty, the radiant, peaceful atmosphere of the home will be conducive to health, happiness, and serenity.

7. Cases of asthma in small children can be caused by emotional conflicts, dissension, and contention between parents. These conflicts generally show up as fear and anxiety in the child, too often bringing on the asthmatic attacks, as well as other ailments.

8. A wonderful prayer for asthma is: "I inhale the peace of God and I exhale the love of God." Repeat frequently and with deep feeling, and believe in the healing power of God.

9. The subconscious may sometimes reveal to you that your healing has taken place through a vivid dream. At the same time you feel subjectively by an inner knowing that you are healed.

10. Your changed attitude of perfect life and health will be transmitted to a sick person, inducing a resurrection of vitality and wholeness in the subconscious mind of the patient.

11. Change your attitude and you change your life. Changed attitudes can change everything! It is done unto you as you believe.

FIFTEEN

The Infinite Power of Love and Your Invisible Matrimonial Guide

God is Life, and Life loves to manifest itself through each of us as harmony, health, peace, joy, abundance, beauty, and right action, or, in other words, life more abundant. There is something in all of us that reminds us of our origin and turns us back to the Source. It is our mission and purpose to enlarge this memory so that it grows from a spark to a flame, and we sense and feel our oneness with God—the Source of all life. There is a deep hunger and thirst in you to unite with the Infinite Source of Life—your Maker.

When you were born you cried for food. As you grew older, you discovered you could never be satisfied without receiving, in addition, spiritual food such as inspiration, guidance, wisdom, and strength from the Infinite Source of all blessings. The Infinite Life Principle is seeking expression through you, and your love for God is expressed by your desire to feel mentally and spiritually united with the Source of all blessings and all power.

Love your mental pictures

Your mental patterns and images are made manifest by your love nature, that is by your emotional attachment. Whatever idea or desire you emotionalize and feel as true is subjectified and made manifest in your world. Make a blueprint for yourself today as you read this chapter, give your attention and devotion to it, adhere to it regularly and systematically, and finally your blueprint will be emotionalized and brought forth into your experience. What you love you become.

At frequent intervals during the day, mentally picture what you want to be, to do, and to have. Do this lovingly, feelingly, but persistently. Do not force or coerce, but with feeling and confidence turn your mental picture over to your subconscious mind, knowing and believing that your subconscious responds to your mental impression.

HOW A WOMAN DREW LASTING LOVE INTO HER LIFE

Recently a young woman asked me, "What is wrong with me? I know I am well educated, I am a business executive, I am a good conversationalist, and many say that I am attractive; yet I attract nothing but married men and alcoholics, and I get shady propositions from others."

Why she was rejecting herself

Her case is typical of a great number of women who are charming, vivacious, lovely, and of excellent character, but they are down on themselves. She had a cruel, despotic, tyrannical father, who never gave her any love or attention. He was the puritanical type, who would not permit her to play games on Sunday, and also forced her to go to church three times every Sunday. Moreover, he quarreled violently with her mother. She felt rejected by her father, who never showed any interest in her school work or general welfare.

She hated him subconsciously and felt guilty about this, which set up a fear in her mind that she should be punished. Constantly arising from the crevasses of her subconscious mind was the feeling that she would be rejected, that she was unworthy of love, and that she was not very attractive.

The mysterious law of attraction

Like attracts like and "birds of a feather flock together." Since her sense of rejection and fear of punishment were a mental state, this automatically attracted to her frustrated, neurotic, inhibited men. The law of mind works and responds negatively or positively according to the thought patterns or directions given it.

How she cleansed
her subconscious mind

At my suggestion she wrote down the following and decided to fill her subconscious mind with the following truths for five or ten minutes in the morning, afternoon, and at night: "I know Divine love dissolves everything unlike itself. I know and believe that what I consciously meditate on is impressed on my subconscious mind and will be expressed in my experience. The Self of me is God. I honor, exalt, and love the God-Self in me. Whenever I am prone to criticize or find fault with myself, I immediately affirm, 'I exalt God in the midst of me.' I forgive myself for harboring resentful and hateful thoughts towards my father, and I wish for him all the blessings of God. Whenever I think of my father, who is now in the next dimension, I bless him. I continue to do this until there is no sting left in my mind. God's love flows through me now. I am surrounded by the peace of God. Divine Love surrounds, enfolds, and encompasses me. This Infinite Love is inscribed in my heart and written in my inward parts. I am radiating love towards all men and women. Divine Love heals me now. Love is a guiding principle in me; it brings into my experience perfect, harmonious relationships. God is love. 'He that dwelleth in love dwelleth in God, and God in him.' "

She continued this prayer therapy process for a month and remained faithful to it. In our next interview, I found a changed young lady. A tremendous transformation had taken place in her mental attitude toward herself, life, and the world in general.

How she made
ready for marriage

She had stopped rejecting herself, a negative attitude which, even though she would have married, would have destroyed the marriage. She prayed as follows: "I believe I can have the ideal husband. I know it is a two-way contract. I give him loyalty, devotion, honesty, integrity, happiness, and fulfillment; and I receive from him loyalty, faith, confidence, trust, love, and fulfillment. The Infinite Intelligence within me knows where the ideal man is and wants fulfillment for me. I am needed, I feel wanted, and I am greatly desired by the man selected by Infinite Intelligence for me. I need him and he needs me. There are harmony, peace, love, and understanding between us. Divine Love unites us, and we harmonize perfectly spiritually, mentally, and physically. I let go of all fears and tensions, and I trust and believe the Infinite Intelligence will bring us together. I know there will be mutual recognition when we meet. He loves me and I love him. I release this whole idea to the Infinite Mind, giving thanks for the Universal Law of Love for its completion now."

She repeated the above prayer with deep feeling night and morning, believing and knowing that these truths were penetrating the walls of her subconscious mind.

How love attracts love

Two months went by. She had several dates; none proved to be of a romantic nature. Whenever she wavered, however, she reminded herself that the Infinite Power was taking care of her request. One day she was flying on business to New York City when a tall, handsome clergyman sat beside her and engaged her in conversation. They discussed various religions, and she discovered that his religious and political beliefs coincided with hers. She attended his church service in New York, and within a week they were engaged. They are now married and live in a beautiful parsonage, where harmony reigns supreme.

HOW A BUSINESSMAN OVERCAME ABNORMAL JEALOUSY WITH LOVE

Love unites; jealousy divides. Milton said, "Jealousy is the injured lover's hell." Shakespeare said, "Oh, beware of jealousy; it is the green-eyed monster, which doth mock the meat it feeds upon." In other words, the jealous man poisons his own banquet, then eats it.

As an example of this, I might tell of a man I knew who had a deep feeling of resentment against a rival in business because of his success, promotion, and popularity. I explained to this man that the deadly venom of jealousy was preying upon all his vital organs, as he had bleeding ulcers, hemorrhoids, and high blood pressure. Moreover, the poison of jealousy generated by him was turning the healthful hue of his face to a haggard sallowness and was devitalizing his whole being.

How the explanation
became the cure

My explanation of the man's difficulties was along these lines: The Infinite Power is one and indivisible. There is no competition, as it cannot compete with itself. There are no divisions or factions in it. There is nothing to oppose it, thwart it, or vitiate it, as it is the only Presence, Power, Cause, and Substance. Certainly the Infinite Being is never in competition with anything or any person. The Infinite Power is the Life-Principle in all men seeking expression through each man in a unique, extraordinary way. There are three billion people in the world, and this Infinite Reservoir of Life is flowing through each person.

Each man can appropriate what he wishes, as the Infinite River of Mind is permeating the mind of all of us. Your thought, your feeling, your attention, and your recognition of this Infinite Power represent your direct pipeline to the Infinite Reservoir. You are the only one in the world who can sever this connection by your lack of belief and faith.

Making the contact with love

You can go within yourself and claim your good, health, wealth, abundance, inspiration, guidance, love, or anything else you want. As you expect and believe, the response will flow in your behalf. You don't want what the other has. Rejoice in his success. You can get what you want by right thinking and feeling. In other words, by establishing the mental equivalent of what you want in your mentality will you reap your reward.

To be jealous of another's talents, success, achievements, or wealth is to demote yourself and attract even more lack, loss, and limitation. Actually, you are rejecting the Divine Source of all good and saying to yourself, "He can have those things and be successful, but I can't." This is ignorance and deprives you of promotion and success. Since there is but one Mind and one Life, you must learn that when in our thought and feeling we sincerely wish for every man, woman, and child in the world the right to life, liberty, happiness, and all the blessings of God, we are truly loving them. Love (goodwill) is the fulfilling of the law of success, happiness, and peace of mind.

How love transformed his life

The above simple and practical discussion about the laws of his mind brought about a new perspective and a new vision of life. The man said to me that he would never again be jealous or resent another man's promotion or success, but that he would rejoice and be glad to learn of any individual's moving onward and upward. I gave him the following prayer to use frequently:

"I know and believe that all of us have one common Progenitor, the Life-Principle, which is the Father of all; and all men are brothers. I salute the Divinity in each person. I know I am shaped and fashioned by what I love. As I pour out love and goodwill to all, I know this purifies and cleanses my subconscious mind of all jealousy, resentment, and fear. I rejoice in the success, promotion, advancement, and happiness of all those around me and of all people everywhere. The river of love and life flows through me, and I am cleansed and at peace."

Whenever a jealous or envious thought came to his mind, he would affirm, "I rejoice in his success. I radiate love and goodwill to him." He made a habit of this, and today he is a wonderful success, operating his own business. The most amazing thing is that the associate of whom he was so terribly jealous is now his partner, and they are prospering beyond their fondest dreams.

HOW TO USE LOVE'S POWER CONSTRUCTIVELY

Some time ago, I interviewed a woman who said, "I have fallen in love with a man. How can I make him propose to me and marry me?" This is the wrong use of the law of love. It is the inversion of love and indicates a desire to mentally coerce or force the other to do something he does not want to do. It is interfering with his God-given privilege and prerogative to choose and decide for himself.

Working mentally on someone else to get him to do what you want is called black magic. This mental power is recognized in India, for example, as well as elsewhere. I explained to her that if she got her man by this means, it would boomerang, and she would wish she had never done it, and, furthermore, that he was not what she really wanted in the first place.

I gave her the following specific prayer for right action:

"The Infinite Intelligence within me knows my desire for marriage. It also knows where the right type of man for me is. He loves me for what I am, and we are mutually attracted. I have no particular man in view as I pray, but I know that the Infinite Mind is now bringing both of us together in Divine order. He comes without encumbrances of any kind, and there are mutual love, interests, and respect. I know and believe 'my own shall come to me.' There is no competition anywhere in life. I give thanks for the Principle of Right Action in my life now, and I know it is done."

She sincerely believed the words she was affirming. She put a feeling of deep conviction into this prayer. After a few weeks, her employer, for whom she had worked five years, proposed to her. They were married and are ideally suited for each other. After the wedding ceremony, which I conducted, she said, "Isn't it funny the way prayer works? I worked in his office for five years, and he never seemed to notice me. Truly, prayer changes things."

Walking in love

Every night and morning dwell mentally on the following, age-old Biblical truths: *God is love* (I John 4:16). *Let all your things be done with charity* (I Cor. 16:14). *Walk in love* (Eph. 5:2). *He that dwelleth in love dwelleth in God* (I John 4:16). *Thou shalt love thy neighbor as thyself* (Lev. 19:18). *For this is the message that ye heard from the beginning, that we should love one another* (I John 3:11). *See that ye love one another with a pure heart fervently* (I Pet. 1:22). *Love worketh no ill to his neighbor; therefore love is the fulfilling of the law* (Rom. 13:10). *Beloved, let us love one another, for love is of God; and every one that loveth is born of God, and knoweth God. He that loveth not knoweth not God; for God is love* (I John 4:7, 8).

POINTS TO RECALL IN THIS CHAPTER

1. Life by its very nature loves to manifest itself as harmony, beauty, joy, and peace; in other words, God's will for you is the abundant life right here and now.

2. Your thought patterns and mental imagery are made manifest in your life by your love nature or your emotional attachment. Whatever idea you emotionalize will come to pass.

3. Cease rejecting yourself. Like attracts like. Realize Divine love dissolves everything unlike itself. If you have a pattern of rejection or a fear complex, fill your subconscious mind with life-giving patterns of harmony, love, peace, joy, and right action; and you will experience a spiritual rebirth.

4. You can attract the ideal spouse by realizing that Cosmic Intelligence within you is now attracting to you the person who harmonizes with you in all ways. Your deeper mind will bring it to pass in Divine order.

5. Jealousy is a mental poison attracting loss, lack, and misery to you. It can be overcome by realizing there is no competition in the one Cosmic Mind. Love casts out jealousy. Whatever you want, you can claim mentally and the God-Presence will give it to you according to your belief in love.

6. Love is an outreaching of the heart. It means goodwill. As you sincerely wish goodwill to others, you will bless yourself, since you are the only thinker in your universe; and what you think about the other is experienced and made manifest in your life. Love is the fulfilling of the law of health, happiness, and peace of mind.

7. Whenever a jealous thought comes to your mind, substitute immediately the following: "I rejoice in the happiness and success of him or her." Make a habit of this, and wonders will happen in your life.

8. Never try to mentally manipulate another to do something he does not want to do. This is an inversion of the law of love, and is called "black magic." Such an act al-

ways boomerangs and brings suffering and regret into your life. To hurt another is to hurt yourself.

9. There is a Principle of Right Action in the universe. The Cosmic Intelligence within you will give you anything you claim, feel, and believe. The Cosmic Mind has billions of channels through which to pour out its infinite blessings. You are a channel of God. Accept your good now.

10. *He that dwelleth in love dwelleth in God* (I John 4:16).

SIXTEEN

The Infinite Power of
Belief to Make the
Impossible Become Possible

The Bible says, *Therefore I say unto you, What things soever ye desire, when ye pray, believe that ye receive them, and ye shall have them* (Mark 11:24). And *Jesus said unto him, if thou canst believe, all things are possible to him that believeth* (Mark 9:23).

To believe is to accept something as true. Great numbers of people, however, believe that which is absolutely false; consequently, they suffer to the extent of their belief. If, for example, you believe that Los Angeles is in Arizona and you address your letter accordingly, it will go astray or be returned to you. Remember that to accept an idea is to actually believe it. If someone suggests to you that you were born to succeed, to become victorious over life's problems, and you accept this completely without any mental reservation, apparent miracles will happen in your life!

THE MIRACLE OF IMPLICIT BELIEVING

When Alexander the Great, the ancient Monarch, was a very young, impressionable boy, his mother, Olympia, told him that his nature was Divine, and that he was different from all other boys, because she had been impregnated by the god Zeus; therefore, he would transcend all the limitations of the average boy. The youth firmly believed this and grew up magnificent in stature, power,

158

and strength; and his life was a series of glorious exploits beyond the comprehension of the average man. He was called "the Divine Lunatic." Alexander was constantly accomplishing both the unpredictable and the impossible. He became an outstanding warrior and conqueror. He accepted completely the belief that he was not the son of his human father, Philip of Macedonia.

It is recorded that at one time he put his arms around a wild, fierce, undisciplined stallion; jumped on it without saddle or bridle; and the horse became as gentle as a lamb. His father and the groom wouldn't dare touch the same horse. However, he believed he was Divine and had power over all animals. He conquered the then known world and established the Alexandrian empire. It is said that he wept because there were no more nations to conquer.

I cite this just to show the power of belief, which enables you to make the so-called impossible possible. *With God all things are possible* (Matt. 19:26). Alexander believed, and dramatized his belief to himself, and made manifest in his own way this Infinite Power in his mind, body, and achievement.

WHY YOU SHOULD KNOW YOU ARE DIVINE

You are a son of the living God. The Bible says, *Call no man your father upon the earth: for one is your Father, which is in heaven* (Matt. 23:9). You are born of God. You are Divine. You have the power, ability, and capacity to do God-like things. *I have said, Ye are gods; and all of you are children of the most High* (Ps. 82:6). Think of all the wonderful things you can accomplish as you call on the Infinite Power within you. Your belief that you are a son of God will set aside all the false beliefs and opinions of man and enable you to do the works of God here and now.

HOW TO ACKNOWLEDGE YOUR DIVINE NATURE

Affirm frequently, "I know and believe I am a son of God, and I am endowed with all the powers, qualities, and attributes of God. I believe implicitly in my Divine nature and I accept my Divine birthright. I am created in the image and likeness of God. I have been given dominion over all things. I can overcome all problems and challenges through the Infinite Power of God within me. Every problem of mine is Divinely outmatched. I definitely believe I can release the Infinite Healing Presence to relieve suffering in myself and in others. I am inspired and illumined from on High. I am expressing more and more of God's love, light, truth, and beauty every day. God is my father, and I know all things are possible to me because I am Divine. I claim this moment that the Light of God shines in me and the glory of God, my Father, is risen upon me. I can do all things through the God-Power, which strengtheneth me."

Continue to reiterate these truths until they become a subjective embodiment, and wonders will happen in your life.

HOW A MINISTER PROVED THE POWER OF BELIEF TO HIMSELF

I had an interesting conversation with a fellow minister a few months ago. He said that his brother, who is an internist and an outstanding diagnostician, had said to him a year previously, "Tom, you have a malignancy." He added, "It was a great shock to me at first." He continued:

"I began to think about what I say in my sermons about God being love and about faith moving mountains, and I said to myself, 'If this be true, why am I so frightened and frustrated? Could it be that I do not really accept these truths, or is it just a theoretical assent on my part?' Suddenly, the thought came to me, if I really believed, I would be alive to the truths of the Bible and honestly live them. I followed the therapy outlined by my brother. The pain was excruciating and I did not respond to the x-ray and drug therapy. I was getting progressively worse. I knew I did not really believe in the Healing Power of God—that these were words and nothing more. I opened the Bible and read these words: *For verily I say unto you, That whosoever shall say unto this mountain, Be thou removed, and be thou cast into the sea; and shall not doubt in his heart, but shall believe that those things which he saith shall come to pass; he shall have whatsoever he saith* (Mark 11:23)."

He meditated on this passage, and the following is the gist of his prayer: "I believe the truths contained in this Biblical verse. The mountain of fear, worry, and ill health is removed and cast into oblivion. This sickness leaves me now. I believe in the Healing Power of God, His goodness, and His care for me. I know that this condition in my body is caused by negative thoughts charged with fear and lodged in my subconscious mind. I know God's healing love is now dissolving and wiping out all negative patterns, and I thank God for the healing that I believe is taking place now. I absolutely refuse to give power to the difficulty, and I rejoice in the truth, *I am the Lord that healeth thee* (Exod. 15:26) .''

He prayed aloud many times a day. When fear and doubt came to his mind, he would immediately affirm, "God is healing me now." At the end of three months all tests proved negative. He is as free as the wind now and is back whole and sound preaching in his church every Sunday and Wednesday, a picture of perfect health.

And all things, whatsoever ye shall ask in prayer, believing, ye shall receive (Matt. 21:22) .

HOW TO BELIEVE IN THE INFINITE HEALING POWER AND BE MADE WHOLE

Through the ages there have been accounts of miraculous spiritual healings. Jesus healed the blind and the lame. He was a man born like all of us. The only difference between Jesus and any other man is that he appropriated more of Divinity by meditating and feasting on the great truths of God, and he had a sense of oneness with God. He said to all men, *The things that I do, ye shall do also, and greater things shall ye do.* He said, also, *And these signs shall follow them that believe . . . they shall cast out devils; they shall speak with new tongues . . . they shall lay hands on the sick, and they shall recover* (Mark 16:17–18) .

The power to heal is in your belief that with God all things are possible.

How a mother made the impossible become possible

I received a phone call from a woman in Louisiana. Her son was in a hospital. He had had a massive cerebral hemorrhage and was not expected to live; he was considered a hopeless case. In talking with this woman, I found she was deeply religious. I asked her, "Do you believe that the Infinite Healing Presence which made his brain and body can heal and restore him?" She replied, "I believe what the Bible says: *For I will restore health unto thee, and I will heal thee of thy wounds, saith the Lord.* (Jer. 30:17) ."

We prayed together over the phone and agreed that the Infinite Healing Power knew how to heal the brain as well as all organs of the body and knew exactly how to repair it. We decreed that an atmosphere of love, peace, and harmony surrounded her son and that all doctors and nurses were Divinely guided in all ways. I suggested to her that she imagine her son home and hear him tell her in her vivid imagination, "Mother, a miracle has happened. I'm completely healed."

The mother continued to pray and believed in the Healing Power of God to restore her son, and she constantly pictured him at home smiling and happy. When fear or any anxious thought came to her mind, she affirmed immediately, "I believe, I believe, I believe in the Infinite Healing Power working a miracle now." This young man is strong and well today!

No one knows exactly how the Healing Presence works. In the same manner, I do not know, nor does anyone know, exactly how a sequoia tree grows from a sequoia seed. This woman absolutely believed that there was an Infinite Intelligence that knew how to heal and repair her son's body. She looked beyond appearances and made the impossible possible.

HOW TO TAKE A TRUE LOOK AT YOUR BELIEFS

Ask yourself, "Does this which I desire exist for me?" Do you believe that you can have wonderful friends and companionship? Do you believe that all the wealth you need is a possibility for you in the universal scheme of things? Do you believe you can find your true place in life? Do you believe that the will of God for you is the abundant life, a greater measure of happiness, peace, joy, prosperity, greater expression and buoyant health? You should answer all these questions affirmatively and believe and expect the best from life, and the best will come to you.

WHAT MANY PEOPLE ERRONEOUSLY BELIEVE ABOUT ABUNDANCE IN THEIR LIVES

Many people think that wealth, happiness, and abundance are not for them, but that these are only for the other person. This is due to a feeling of inferiority or rejection. *There is no such thing as an inferior or a superior person.* Everyone is a god, though in the germ: *Ye are gods; and all of you are children of the most High* (Ps. 82:6).

You are not limited by family, race, or early conditioning. There are thousands of people who have transcended their environments and have raised their heads and shoulders above the crowd, although they were not born with gold spoons in their mouths. Abraham Lincoln was born in a log cabin; Jesus was the son of a carpenter; George Carver, the great scientist, was born into slavery. The universal bounty of God, however, is poured out on all regardless of race, creed, or color.

It is done unto you as you believe. If you don't believe that you have the right to your heart's desire, knowing that the law is impersonal, always responding to your belief, you can't believe you will have your desire!

YOU HAVE THE RIGHT TO BELIEVE IN RICH AND JOYOUS LIVING

God, Cosmic Good, gave you richly all things to enjoy, and you are placed here to glorify God and enjoy Him forever. You have the perfect right to bring any good into your life provided your motive is unselfish and that you wish for everyone what you wish for yourself. Your desire for health, happiness, peace, love, and abundance cannot possibly harm anyone. You have the right to a wonderful position with a marvelous income, but you should not covet any other person's job. The Infinite Presence can guide you to right employment with an income consistent with your integrity and honesty.

Believe you have the right to the good you seek and do everything you know to bring it into your experience, and then it will manifest. You don't want anything which some other person is enjoying. God's infinite riches are available to all. Life responds to you according to your belief in It and your use of It.

YOU GET WHAT YOU BELIEVE

All of your experiences, conditions, and events grow out of your beliefs. Cause and effect are indissolubly united and linked together. Your habitual thinking finds its expression in all phases of your life. Believe you have a Silent Partner who comforts you, guides and directs you, and who holds before you an open door which no man can shut. Live in the joyous expectancy of the best, and invariably the best will come to you.

Every morning when you wake, affirm quietly and lovingly: "This is the day which the Lord hath made. I will rejoice and be glad in it. Wonders will happen in my life today. I will make marvelous contacts today. I will meet wonderful and most interesting people. I will complete all my assignments in Divine order, and I will accomplish great things today. My Silent Partner reveals to me new and better ways to accomplish all things. I know the Infinite Power sees no obstacles, knows no barriers. I believe God is prospering me beyond my wildest dreams. I know and believe that . . . *all things are possible to him that believeth* (Mark 9:23) ."

HOW A BANKRUPT MAN CLAIMED HIS GOOD

Some time ago I interviewed a man who had gone bankrupt. He was depressed and dejected. Furthermore, his wife had divorced him and his children no longer contacted him. He said that his wife had poisoned their minds against him. He commented that he did not believe in God and that he was at the end of the rope.

I pointed out to him that even if he believed the world is flat, nevertheless, it is still round. Furthermore, there is Infinite Intelligence within a man whether he believes there is or not. I suggested to him that he try a formula for ten days, and at the end of that time come back and see me. The formula I gave him was as follows:

"I believe that God is, and that God is the Infinite Power that moves the world and created all things. I believe this Infinite Power indwells me. I believe God is guiding me now. I believe God's riches flow to me in avalanches of abundance. I believe God's love fills my heart and that His love fills the minds and hearts of my two boys. I believe that the bonds of love and peace unite us. I believe I am a tremendous success. I believe I am happy, joyous, and free. I believe God is always successful, and because God is successful and because God indwells me, I am a tremendous success. I believe, I believe, I believe."

I suggested that he affirm the above truths out loud five minutes morning, afternoon, and night. He agreed, and the second day he phoned and said, "I don't believe a word of what I am saying. It's all mechanical and has no meaning." I told him to persist in this mental discipline. "The mere fact that you started to affirm and practice the spiritual formula indicates the faith of a grain of mustard seed mentioned in the Bible; and, as you keep it up, you will remove the mountains of fear, lack, and frustration."

He came back at the end of ten days radiant and happy. His two sons had visited him, and there was a joyous reunion. In his new pattern of thought, he won a small fortune on the Irish Sweepstakes and is now back in business. He discovered that the Infinite Power for perfect living also applied to him!

I knew that even though the words of the prayer meant nothing to him as he started, as he continued to dwell upon them through frequent habitation of the mind, they would sink into his subconscious mind and become a part of his mentality.

. . . for verily I say unto you, If ye have faith as a grain of mustard seed, ye shall say unto this mountain, Remove hence to yonder place; and it shall remove; and nothing shall be impossible unto you (Matt. 17:20).

POINTS TO RECALL IN THIS CHAPTER

1. The Bible says, . . . *if thou canst believe, all things are possible to him that believeth* (Mark 9:23).
2. To believe is to accept something as true. You can believe a lie, but you can't prove it. If you believe something which is false, you will suffer to the extent of your belief.

3. Alexander the Great was told by his mother that she was impregnated by the god Zeus. Alexander accordingly believed his nature was Divine. Consequently, he believed he could accomplish, and did accomplish, what other men believed impossible.

4. Believe you are a son of the Living God and that you are endowed with the Infinite Power and qualities of God. Continue in this belief and you will work miracles in your life. Believe you can do all things through the God Power which strengtheneth you.

5. If you say to the mountain (the obstacle, difficulty, problem) be thou removed and be thou cast into the sea of oblivion and believe that the Infinite Power of God can do this, it shall come to pass.

6. Take a Biblical quotation such as, *I am the Lord that healeth thee* (Exod. 15:26). Reiterate this truth in your mind regularly and believe in the Infinite Healing Presence, and a healing will follow. It is done unto you as you believe.

7. Believe that with the Infinite Healing Power all things are possible.

8. Believe that the Infinite Power which made your body and created all your organs can repair it and restore it to wholeness. Claim it, and saturate your mind with this great truth: *I will restore health unto thee, and I will heal thee of thy wounds, saith the Lord* (Jer. 30:17). By recalling this truth frequently, you will reach a point of inner peace, and a healing will follow.

9. Look beyond appearances and contemplate the reality of the wish fulfilled, and you will make the impossible possible.

10. Take a look at your beliefs and recast them in the light of the great affirmatives. Believe in the goodness of God, in the guidance of God, and in the life more abundant.

11. You are divinely entitled to all the riches of life. God is the giver and the gift, and all things be ready if the mind be so. Accept your good now and live in the joyous expectancy of the best. You are not limited by family, race, or early training.

12. God gave you richly all things to enjoy. You are here to glorify God and enjoy Him forever. God's infinite riches

are available to all. Life responds to you according to your belief in It and your use of It.

13. All your experiences, conditions, and events grow out of your belief.

14. If you affirm that you do not believe in universal principles and the truths of God, and at the same time you begin to affirm that what is true of God is true of you, the mere fact that you begin to affirm the truth is the faith of a grain of mustard seed, which expands and grows as you continue to reiterate and announce these truths to your mind. You will discover that belief works wonders and even miracles in your life.

SEVENTEEN

Infinite Power for Harmonious Relationships with People

This chapter is being written on the beautiful island of Maui, one of the chain comprising the state of Hawaii. The people here say, "You have not lived until you have seen Hawaii." One of Maui's outstanding attractions is Haleakula, "House of the Sun," an extinct volcano, which rises more than ten thousand feet. It offers views of breathtaking scenery and a glimpse of quiet native life where Hawaiians still cast nets into the sea for essential food and tend taro patches in the manner of their ancestors.

In these islands you meet people of every ethnic group and of diverse religious beliefs living together harmoniously, peacefully, and enjoying the sunshine of God's love. The native who drove me from the airport to Maui Hilton Hotel told me that his antecedents were a mixture of Irish, Portuguese, German, Japanese, and Chinese. He pointed out that the people here have intermarried for generations and that racial problems are unknown.

HOW TO GET ALONG WITH OTHERS

One of the chief reasons some men and women do not get ahead in life is their inability to get along with others. They seem to "rub" others the wrong way. Often their attitude of pomposity is tactless and offensive. The best way to get along with others is to salute the Divinity in the other person and to realize that every

168

man and woman is an epitome or example of the entire human race. Every person who walks the earth is a son or daughter of the Living God; and when we respect and honor the Divinity within ourselves, we will automatically revere and honor the Divine Presence in the other person.

HOW A WAITER PROMOTED HIMSELF

While visiting one of the chain of hotels in the Koanapali Beach district of Maui, I had an interesting conversation with a waiter. He told me that every year an eccentric millionaire from the mainland visited the hotel. This visitor proved to be a miserly type who hated to give a waiter or a bellboy a tip. He was churlish, ill-mannered, rude, and just plain ornery. Nothing satisfied him, and he was constantly complaining about the food and the service, and he snarled at the waiter whenever he served him. This waiter said to me, "I realized he was a sick man. Our Kahuna (a native Hawaiian priest) says that when men are like that there is something eating their insides, so I decided to kill him with kindness."

How the special technique worked wonders

This waiter consistently treated this man with courtesy, kindness and respect, silently affirming, "God loves him. I see God in him and he sees God in me." He practiced this technique for about a month, at the end of which time this eccentric millionaire for the first time said, "Good morning, Toni. How's the weather? You're the best waiter I have ever had." Toni told me, "I almost fainted; I expected a growl and I got a compliment. He gave me a five hundred dollar bill." This was a parting tip from this difficult guest, who at the same time arranged for Toni to be made an assistant manager eventually of a large hotel in Honolulu, in which he was financially interested.

And a word spoken in due season, how good is it! (Prov. 15:23) .

A word is a thought expressed. This waiter's words (thoughts) were addressed to the soul (subconscious mind) of the cranky, cantankerous guest, they gradually melted the ice in his heart, and he responded in love and kindness. Toni proved that seeing the Presence of God in the other and adhering to that great eternal truth pays fabulous dividends in human relations, spiritually as well as materially.

TO UNDERSTAND ALL IS TO FORGIVE ALL

This is an old aphoristic statement containing a profound truth. I had an interesting conversation with a social director in one of the hotels here in Maui. She pointed out that occasionally when she says to a guest, "It's a wonderful day," the guest says, "What's good about it? I hate the weather here, I don't like anything about the place." She added that she knew that particular guest was emotionally disturbed and driven by some irrational emotion. She had studied psychology at the University of Hawaii in Honolulu and remembered that her teacher had pointed out to her that one does not get upset or resentful toward a person who is a hunchback, for example, or who suffers from any other obvious congenital deformity; likewise, one should not be disturbed because some people are emotional hunchbacks and have twisted and disturbed mentalities. One should have compassion for them. Understanding their mental and emotional chaotic state, it is easy to overlook and forgive them.

How understanding builds immunity to hard feelings

This young lady is gracious, charming, affable and amiable, and apparently nobody can "ruffle her feathers." She has built up a sort of Divine immunity, and she fully realizes that no one can hurt her but herself. That is to say, she has freedom, as anyone has, to bless the other person or to resent the other person. She has decided to bless. She knows very well that the only one able to hurt her is she herself, i.e., the movement of her own thought, which is under her complete control.

HOW A MUSICIAN'S SUBCONSCIOUS WORKED WONDERS FOR HIM THROUGH PRAYER

A young musician who plays a stringed instrument at night to pay his way through the University of Hawaii where he is studying law told me that he had experienced friction with some of his teachers and that his memory had failed him during the oral and written examinations. This young man was tense and resentful. I explained to him that his subconscious mind contained a perfect memory of everything he had read and heard but that when his conscious mind is tense, the wisdom of the subconscious does not rise to the surface mind.

Accordingly, he prayed as follows every night and morning: "Infinite Intelligence in my subconscious mind reveals to me everything I need to know, and I am Divinely guided in my studies. I radiate love and goodwill to my teachers and I am at peace with them. I pass all my examinations in Divine order."

Three weeks went by and I received a letter from him saying he had passed his special examination with flying colors and that his relationship with his teachers is now excellent.

He succeeded in incorporating the idea of perfect memory for everything he needed to know into his subconscious mind by reiterating the affirmations I gave him. His emanation of love and goodwill was subconsciously picked up by his teachers, resulting in harmonious relationships.

HOW A DOCTOR HEALED HIMSELF
OF CRIPPLING ANGER

Haleakala Crater, once a fiery, gaping depression, is now a cool, cone-studded aftermath of a violent volcano. I was with a group of people, some of whom were from such widely diverse localities as Denver; Pittsburgh; Stockholm, Sweden; and Australia. I sat next to an Australian doctor and his wife in the limousine. He told me that volcanic eruptions causing havoc similar to the results of the volcanic activity at which we were looking had taken place in his life because he was in the habit of judging people too harshly.

The gist of his conversation was that he used to boil over with rage at what the columnists wrote in the newspapers. He wrote poisonous, vindictive and vitriolic letters to members of parliament, to heads of the various unions, etc. This internal seething and turmoil brought on two physical eruptions in two severe cardiac attacks plus one volcanic eruption in the form of a mild stroke.

He recovered from these attacks and realized that he had brought them on himself. While in the hospital, a nurse gave him the 91st Psalm to read, saying, "This is the medicine you need." He began to dwell on it, and gradually its meaning sank into his soul (his subconscious mind). He pointed out that he had long since learned to adjust to people, realizing that they are all conditioned differently and that this is a world of imperfect human beings striving toward God's Perfection.

What being true
to inner self means

This doctor had learned to be true, as he said, to the God-Self within him and to respect the same God in the other. Shakespeare said, "To thine own self be true; then it follows, as the night the day, thou canst not be false to any man." This doctor had learned that to understand all is to forgive all. He is still intolerant of false ideas, but not people. He remains true to the truths of God and eternal principles.

HOW A MAN WITH A GRUDGE AGAINST GOD LEARNED
A GREAT LESSON IN HUMAN RELATIONS

A man with whom I went swimming in the ocean adjacent to the beautiful and majestic Maui Hilton Hotel said to me, "I'm here to get away from it all." He began to criticize everybody in his organization, as well as the government; he even seemed to have a grudge against God. In fact, he told me he felt he would get along better if God would just let him alone.

He asked me, "What can I do to have better human relations and get along with these ugly people?" I suggested to him that research has demonstrated that much of the difficulty many people have in human relations is that they don't look within themselves for the cause. The first step would be to get along with his own difficult self. I pointed out to him that much of his trouble with his employees and associates came from himself primarily and that these other people might be called secondary causes.

He admitted he was full of hidden rage and hostility and was deeply frustrated in his ambitions and plans in life. He began to see, however, that his suppressed rage kindled the latent hostility or anger in those around him; and he suffered from their reactions, which he himself had engendered. He discovered that what he termed the animosity and hostility of his associates and employees reflected his own hostility and frustration to a great extent.

I gave him a spiritual prescription, which he was to follow regularly and systematically: "I know that there is a law of cause and effect, and the mood which I generate is returned to me in the reactions of people to me and in conditions and events. I realize my inner turmoil and anger sets off ugliness and anger in men and women and, also, animals. I know that no matter what I experience, it must have an affinity in my mind, conscious or unconscious; for as I think and feel, so am I, and so do I express, experience and behave.

"I give myself this mental and spiritual medicine many times a day. I think, speak and act from the Divine Center within me. I radiate love, peace and goodwill to all those around me and to all people everywhere. The Infinite lies stretched in smiling repose within me. Peace is the power at the heart of God, and His river of peace floods my mind, my heart, and my whole being. I am one with the Infinite peace of God. My mind is a part of God's mind, and what is true of God is true of me.

"I realize and know that no person, place or thing in the whole world has the power to upset, annoy or disturb me without my mental consent. My thought is creative; and I consciously and knowingly reject all negative thoughts and suggestions, affirming that God is my guide, my counselor and my governor and that He watches over me. I know God is my real Employer and I am working for Him.

"The real Self of me is God and cannot be hurt, vitiated or thwarted. I realize I am the one who has hurt myself the most by my self-criticism, self-condemnation and self-denigration. I send kindness, love and joy to all people; and I know goodness, truth and beauty follow me all the days of my life, for I live in the house of God forever."

Three weeks transpired; and he wrote me, saying that practicing this phase of mental and spiritual laws had replaced his inner chaotic, seething cauldron state of mind with serenity, tranquility and a sense of imperturbability.

HOW A BENEFICIAL PHILOSOPHICAL ATTITUDE TOWARD PEOPLE WAS DEVELOPED

I had an interesting conversation with a Japanese businessman in Hawaii, who philosophized along these lines: "I have been in business 50 years and have traveled extensively. I have learned that people are basically good and honest. I take people as they come. They are all different: they have had different training and conditioning; they have different customs and religious beliefs; and they are the result of their training, education and habitual thinking.

"I know complaining about people and getting angry with customers won't change them. I don't let them disturb me; I refuse to let anybody get under my skin. I bless them all and walk on."

How collections of
unpaid bills were made

He showed me a list of ten customers who owed him considerable sums of money and who had ignored his several bills. He said, "I have been praying for each one, morning and night, realizing God is prospering them in all ways and that God guides, directs and multiplies their good. I pray that each pays his bills gladly and that they are honest, sincere and blessed in all ways. I started a month ago doing this; and eight of them have paid, apologizing for the delay. There are two to go, but I know they will pay, too."

He discovered that when he changed his mental attitude toward the delinquent customers, they changed, also.

THE KEY TO HAPPY RELATIONS

Treat people with respect. Honor and salute the Divinity in the other. Radiate love and goodwill to all. Realize that nobody acts in a contentious, hostile, antagonistic and surly manner who is well adjusted. Know there is a mental conflict somewhere. As the Kahuna says, "There is something eating them inside." There is a psychic pain somewhere. God is the true Self of you. It can't be hurt, thwarted or vitiated in any way. If you find difficult people in your life, surrender them to God, declare your freedom in God and let God take them under His care. You will then find yourself in green pastures and beside still waters.

POINTS TO RECALL IN THIS CHAPTER

1. One of the chief reasons some men and women do not get ahead in daily life is their inability to get along with others.
2. Realize every person who walks the earth is a son or daughter of God. As you honor and respect the God-Self within, you will automatically honor the Divine Presence in the other.
3. A waiter handling a churlish, ill-mannered and rude customer who snarled at him, realized the man was mentally sick and consequently treated him with kindness, courtesy and respect. Every time he waited on him, he affirmed, "God loves him." The waiter's attitude melted the ice in the heart of his customer, paying the waiter dividends in promotion and wealth.
4. To understand all is to forgive all. When you understand the cause of the inner turmoil of others, you become more compassionate and understanding. You understand he acts the way he does because of his training, indoctrination and conditioning.
5. Learn that no one can hurt your feelings or "ruffle your feathers" except through the movement of your own thought, which is under your complete control.
6. Friction, inner turmoil and anger will interfere with your studies and memory, as the wisdom of the deeper mind will not rise to the conscious mind when the latter is tense and antagonistic. Pour out love and goodwill on others until you meet them in your mind and you are at peace.
7. Intense rage and anger can cause heart attacks and other destructive conditions. To neutralize these noxious emotions, dwell on the truths of the 91st Psalm, letting them sink into the subconscious mind and thereby banishing

hostility and suppressed rage. Remain faithful to the truths of God within you, and you will walk in pleasantness and paths of peace.

8. The first step to establishing a good relationship with people is to look within yourself and ask, "Might it be possible that the hostility and animosity of others toward me reflect my own hostility and frustration to a great extent?" Change yourself and you will change your relationship with people.

9. There is a law of cause and effect always operating. The mood you generate is returned to you in the reactions of people and in conditions and events in your life.

10. Learn to take people as they come and do not try to change them. People act according to their training, conditioning and habitual thinking. Bless them and go about your affairs.

11. If people owe you money, pray for their prosperity, success and happiness. Realize they are honest, sincere and will pay all their debts in Divine order.

12. The key to harmonious relations with people is to have a healthy, reverent respect for the Divinity within yourself and at the same time respect and salute the Divinity in the other person.

13. If a person is very difficult to get along with, surrender him to God completely and declare your freedom in God. The unpleasantness will disappear from your experience. *Thou shalt also decree a thing and it shall be established unto thee . . .* (Job 22:28).

EIGHTEEN

The Benefits of Traveling with God

I went on a lecture tour recently in Europe, visiting Portugal, France, England and Ireland. As I traveled east from California, on alighting from the plane in New York City, I met an old friend, Jack Treadwell, author of a popular book, *The Laws of Mental Magnetism*.[1] He told me of an elderly man in the hotel where he lived who had been crippled with arthritis. He had suggested to him that he try prayer therapy, and he gave him a special prayer to use: "God's Healing Love is now transforming every atom of my being into God's pattern of wholeness, beauty and perfection."

This man affirmed these truths for ten or fifteen minutes every day. At the end of a month he was walking freely, joyously and easily. All the calcareous deposits, which cause arthritis, were eliminated. He had decided to travel with God mentally, spiritually and physically.

There is nothing miraculous in this healing. The Infinite Healing Presence which created his body had always been within him, but he had failed to use it. Jack Treadwell taught him how to stir up this gift of God within him. This is what the Bible means when it says: *Wherefore I put thee in remembrance that thou stir up the gift of God, which is in thee . . .* (II Tim. 1:6). When you walk, talk and travel with God, everything unlike God is dissolved in your mind, body and circumstances.

---

[1] Jack Treadwell, *The Laws of Mental Magnetism* (West Nyack, N.Y.: Parker Publishing Co., 1965).

HOW TO TRAVEL WITH GOD

Whenever I take a trip or go on a lecture tour, I pray as follows: "My journey is God's journey, and all His ways are pleasantness and all his paths are peace. I travel under God's guidance led by the Holy Spirit. My highway is the Royal Road of the Ancients, the middle path of Buddha, the straight and narrow gate of Jesus, the King's Highway, for I am a King over all my thoughts, feelings and emotions. I send my messengers called God's love, peace, light and beauty before me to make straight, beautiful, joyous and happy my way. I always travel with God, meeting His messengers of peace and joy wherever I go. I know that with mine eyes stayed on God, there is no evil on my pathway.

"While traveling on an airplane, bus, train, car or by foot, God's spell is always around me. It is the invisible armor of God, and I go from point to point freely, joyously and lovingly. The Spirit of God is upon me, making all roads in the heavens above or on the earth beneath a highway for my God. It is wonderful!"

Why many seem to
lead a charmed life

I have given the preceding prayer to hundreds of people who travel overseas, and they really lead a charmed life by saturating their minds and hearts with the above truths, which sink into their subconscious minds, and their deeper mind responds accordingly. *Thy faith hath saved thee; go in peace* (Luke 7:50) .

CAN YOU BELIEVE IN MIRACLES?

My first stop after leaving New York was Lisbon. Portugal is a land of rugged mountains, rolling plains, cork farms and thirteenth and fourteenth century hamlets. I hired a car with a special guide, and together with a niece of mine from Liverpool, journeyed to the shrine of Fatima. Our guide explained the story of Fatima by stating that the Blessed Virgin had appeared to three children on the thirteenth of May, 1917. Their names were Lucia,

Francisco and Jacinta. A sudden flash of lightning had surrounded the children, and as they looked towards the tree, they saw upon it the figure of "Our Lady" brighter than the sun. Lucia had asked the "Lady" who she was, and the reply had been, "I am from Heaven. Return here six times at this same hour on the thirteenth day of every month."

The children had been pestered and accused of lying; however, thousands had believed them. But only the children could see the Blessed Virgin. Sick people had been cured and miracles of healing had taken place at the purported place of the "Lady's" appearance.

The final appearance of "Our Lady" had taken place on the thirteenth of October. It was raining and a flash of lightning announced that the Blessed Virgin had appeared. She predicted that the war, then in its third year, would soon end, and also made other prophetic pronouncements. Our guide said that on that day about 40,000 people had witnessed the dancing of the sun. The rain had suddenly stopped and all the people had fallen to their knees as they had seen the sun surrounded by a shining crown, bursting and turning around like a wheel of fireworks.

A healing observed first hand

We visited the Chapel of the Apparitions. Our guide pointed out to us a woman whose right leg was paralyzed. She was on crutches and accompanied by her son. Our guide interpreted her prayer, which was in Portuguese, as follows: "When I kneel down where the Virgin appeared, I will be healed, praise God." We watched her as she knelt with one knee, holding a rosary in her hand. She prayed fervently to the Virgin, and in about fifteen minutes we saw her get up and walk freely out of the chapel with tears of joy in her eyes. The Bible says: . . . *If thou canst believe, all things are possible to him that believeth* (Mark 9:23) .

THE MEANING OF A MIRACLE

A miracle is not a violation of natural law. A miracle does not prove that which is impossible; it proves that which is possible. A miracle is something that happens when one brings in a higher law than those which man has known heretofore.

Cause of her healing

The woman referred to above was healed by her belief and expectancy. She believed that if she could only be in the place where she believed that the Virgin had appeared, she would be healed. Her belief released the healing power of her own subconscious mind! The law of life is the law of belief, and belief could be briefly summed up as a thought in your mind. To believe is to accept something as true. Whatever your conscious, reasoning mind accepts as true engenders a corresponding reaction from your subconscious mind, which is one with the Infinite Intelligence within you. This woman's blind faith or belief healed her.

THE INFINITE HEALING POWER AND HOW TO USE IT

The true method of spiritual healing does not lie in some magic, such as wand-waving, visiting shrines, touching relics, bathing in certain waters or kissing the bones of saints, but rather in the mental response of man to the Indwelling Infinite Healing Presence which created him and all things in the world.

Spiritual healing and
faith healing not the same

Spiritual healing is not the same as faith healing. A faith healer may be any person who heals without any knowledge or scientific understanding of the powers of the conscious and subconscious mind. He may claim that he has some magical gift of healing, and the sick person's blind belief in his or her powers may bring results.

The spiritual therapist must know what he is doing and why he is doing it. He trusts the law of healing. The law of mind is that whatever you impress on your subconscious mind will be expressed in like manner as form, function, experience and events.

THE MEANING OF THE APPEARANCE OF
THE BLESSED VIRGIN

The name of the Virgin is frequently referred to as Mary. The Latin word "mare" means the sea. The word "virgin" means pure, and "virgin mare" means pure sea. It means the female aspect of God. This female aspect or subjective mind is referred to in ancient symbolism as Isis, whose veil no man may lift; as Sophia of the Persians; as Diana of the Ephesians; and she is also called Istar Astarte, Mylitta and Maya, the mother of Buddha. The term "Mother of God" usually refers to the Madonna. Of course, God has no father or mother. God is the Life-Principle which was never born and will never die. The "Mother of God" means to mother, dwell on or nourish that which is good in your mind. It is a mental attitude. The "Mother of God" or the "Madonna" or "Our Lady" is a pure myth, which is a projected psychological truth meaning love, beauty, order, the mind that gives birth to God or all things good.

Were apparitions at Lourdes
and Fatima subjective
creations of mind?

If I hypnotized you and while you were in the hypnotic state suggested to you that on bringing you out of the trance you would see your grandmother and talk to her and that she would give you prophetic announcements for yourself and the world, your subconscious mind would project the image of your grandmother, and you would see her and talk to her. Your subconscious would utter predictions and prognostications based on the nature of my suggestion. Remember, there is a memory picture of your grandmother in your subconscious mind. It would not be your real grandmother, who undoubtedly is busy in the next dimension of life. You would have simply experienced a subjective hallucination. The others present in the room where you were hypnotized could not see your grandmother; you would be the only one capable of seeing your projected thought picture. At Fatima it was reported that it was only the *children who saw the Virgin; the multitude did not.*

Bernadette's Vision at Lourdes

According to some authorities, Bernadette's early life was lonely. She suffered from asthmatic attacks and was emotionally inhibited. The excitation and expectancy of her mind that she would see "Our Lady" acted as an auto-hypnotic suggestion, and her subconscious mind projected a picture of a woman which conformed with the statue in her church or the picture of the Virgin in her prayer book. Her experiences seem to be projected from within her own mind. Hallucinations are based on the conditioning of your mind. Anyone who fervently desires to see a saintly being can condition his subconscious to see *his concept* of the Virgin Mary or any other personage, based on statues, prayer book pictures or paintings of same.

WHY THE PROPHECIES CAME TO PASS

The Lady at Fatima told Jacinta and Francisco that they would die of influenza and that Lucia would become a nun. All this happened. Remember, your future is already in your mind, and a capable psychic or medium can also predict your future with a fair degree of accuracy. Your future is your present state of mind made manifest, but by prayer you can change the future by thinking from the standpoint of universal principles. Change your thought life to conform to harmony, health, peace, love, right action, and Divine law and order, and all your ways will be pleasantness and all your paths will be peace. Then, any negative prediction cannot come to pass. In this case, it was the children's own subconscious which guided the predictions to come true.

The basis of miracles
as observed in Europe

There was much turbulence, strife and rioting during my trip to Paris, but I received a pleasant reception from Dr. Mary Sterling and her associates. She is the Director of Unite Universelle, 22 Rue De Douai, Paris, and has translated many of my books into French. She has a prayer group at her center, and they achieve amazing healings and answers to prayer. Requests come from all over France. I spoke to a very large and distinguished group of men and women there and received a memorable ovation.

The basis of a
healing of blindness

A young woman who attended one of my lectures in Paris visited me at the Hotel Napoleon about an emotional problem, and in the course of conversation she told me that when she first came to Paris from one of the provinces she was employed as a dressmaker. Her employers were cruel and mean to her. She resented them very much, and subsequently she found herself losing her vision. She went to an opthalmologist and he suggested she give up dressmaking and go back to the country life. She refused and her sight got worse. She went to see a local medical doctor and he told her to quit her position and find another, that her subconscious mind was trying to shut out the unpleasant surroundings and her employers. She did this. She found another position where she was happy, and her vision was gradually restored.

She told me that she actually hated the sight of her former employers. Then, of course, her subconscious responded by seeing to it that she couldn't see them or her surroundings. She finally learned to bless her former employers and walk on.

In the case of failing eyesight, it is wise to ask yourself why your subconscious mind is making your eyes the scapegoat. What is it in your life you wish to exclude or shut out? The answer is within you and so is the solution.

Her Divine Companion
saved her life

A French newspaperwoman met me at the Orly Airport, because there were no taxis operating in Paris due to a strike. She is an old friend of mine and constantly uses the same prayer I use in traveling and which I included in the first part of this chapter. She said that this special prayer was as much a part of her as her hair.

Last year she was about to take a trip to North Africa, Greece and some other Mediterranean countries. One night, she said, I appeared to her in a dream and told her to wait—postpone the trip—as the plane she was going on would meet with disaster. She cancelled the trip, and the plane in question crashed. She told me that she understood the way her deeper mind worked; i.e., her subconscious mind projected an image of a person she trusted and would obey. Actually, it was the God-Presence within her which protected her. Her Divine Companion watched over her in all her ways. This is the Presence of God in all of us. . . . *I the Lord will make myself known unto him in a vision, and will speak unto him in a dream* (Num. 12:6) .

HOW TO USE THE POWER OF YOUR SUBCONSCIOUS MIND TO MAKE A FORTUNE

Dr. Mary Sterling informed me that the sale of her French translation of *The Power of Your Subconscious Mind*[2] is exceeding all expectations and that many letters are pouring into her sanctuary at 22 Rue De Douai, Paris, attesting to remarkable healings and answers to prayer. One Parisian told me that he has made a fortune by following a technique outlined in the French edition of my book, by affirming for about ten minutes prior to sleep "Wealth is mine; wealth is mine now" over and over again until he lulled himself to sleep. He succeeded by repetition in impregnating his mind, and he said everything he touched seemed to be like the touch of Midas—he has made a fortune. In one instance he won a lottery worth $60,000 in American money. He sincerely believes in the power of his subconscious to guide, direct, heal and inspire him, and it responded according to his belief.

THERE IS ALWAYS AN ANSWER

While I was traveling to London from Paris for a series of lectures in Caxton Hall, London, and also Bournemouth, a seaside

---

2 Joseph Murphy, *The Power of Your Subconscious Mind* (Englewood Cliffs, N.J.: Prentice-Hall, Inc., 1963) .

resort in the south of England, a French girl sat beside me and said, "I am going to London to listen to your lectures, as I want to hear more about the powers of my mind. During one of your lectures in Paris, you said that whatever you impressed on your subconscious mind would be expressed and fulfilled." Then she added that she decreed, "I am going to London in Divine order to listen to a series of lectures by Dr. Murphy and everything will be provided by my deeper mind." She happened to speak to her brother, who is a medical doctor in Paris, about her interest in the subconscious mind, and he said to her, "Sis, why don't you go to London and take in the series of lectures?" He gave her about two thousand francs—more than enough for the trip—whereas she had previously thought that her brother was hostile to this teaching.

The ways of your subconscious are past finding out. She discovered, as thousands of others have done, that there is always an answer. . . . *Seek, and ye shall find; knock, and it shall be opened unto you* (Matt. 7:7) . I might add that this young girl was going to school and had no money of her own.

How a person won on the English Derby three times

During one of my lectures at Caxton Hall, London, where I have given a series of lectures about every two years for the past twenty years, and in an area where I enjoy a host of friends, a young man spoke to me, saying, "I hope you don't think I'm using my mind the wrong way, but three months before our annual derby race, every night I affirm before sleep, 'The winner in the derby,' and I lull myself to sleep with the one word 'winner,' knowing that my subconscious will reveal to me the answer." For three consecutive years he has seen the winner the night before the race in a dream, and last year he bet one thousand pounds, which won him a handsome sum of money. His subconscious responded to his faith in its powers. His preview of the race is called precognition, which is a faculty of the mind.

I explained to him that the subconscious is amoral; it is a law, and a law is neither good nor bad. It depends on how you use it. There is nothing wrong in seeing the questions in the subconscious in an examination prior to taking it; there is nothing wrong in seeing the winner of a dog or a horse race, either. There is only one subjective mind, and it is in the dog, the cat and in all other things as well.

HOW DISSOLVING GUILT HEALED AN ULCERATED ARM

A young surgeon visited me at St. Ermine's Hotel next to Caxton Hall, a lecture hall. He had just listened to one of my lectures on "Why You Can Be Healed." He showed me his arm, which was badly ulcerated. He had tried all manner of therapy to no avail—the ulcer refused to respond. I asked him what he had done with his right hand that might have caused a sense of guilt, and he replied honestly and with sadness, "When I was an intern, I performed several abortions for monetary reasons. According to my religion that is murder, and I feel guilty and full of remorse." I asked him, "Would you do it now?" He said, "Of course not. I am helping people to get well now."

I told him that he was punishing himself; that the man who performed these operations no longer existed, inasmuch as every atom of his body changes every eleven months. Moreover, he was completely changed mentally, emotionally and spiritually, and he was actually condemning an innocent man. God condemns no one, and when we forgive ourselves we are forgiven. Self-condemnation is indeed hell—self-forgiveness is heaven.

This surgeon immediately saw the point. The past was dead. He saw himself as innocent. Before the end of my week's lectures, he showed me his hand and arm which had become completely whole and perfect. Paul said, . . . *This one thing I do, forgetting those things which are behind, and reaching forth unto those things which are before, I press toward the mark for the prize* . . . (Phil. 3:13, 14).

"Kevin of the Miracles"

Glendaloch is traditionally known as the site of the "Seven Churches" in Ireland. St. Kevin spent about four years of incredible austerity here, living on herbs, roots and berries found locally. He was born in 498 and died in 618. He is called "Kevin of the Miracles."

A local farmer was accidentally struck in the eye by a stone. The man lost the sight of the affected eye and suffered excruciating pain. St. Kevin touched the injured eye with a fervent invocation to God. At once the wound healed, the flow of blood ceased and the pain vanished. The man's sight was restored. It is said that this miracle was witnessed by many members of the community, who were greatly edified as a result.

A place of pilgrimage

A visit to St. Kevin's bed is an essential part of the pilgrimage to Glendaloch. The bed is a cavity in the rock about thirty feet above water level. There is a traditional promise that those who succeed in climbing into St. Kevin's bed will have their dearest wish granted. There is an extra wish granted to those who decide to sit in St. Kevin's chair.

My sister accompanied me on this pilgrimage to St. Kevin's, and we talked to a woman who was on the pilgrimage from Killarney. She told us that some years ago she had been in the terminal stages of cancer; her guide had aided her in reaching St. Kevin's bed in the rock, and she had prayed there to St. Kevin. A few days later she felt healed, and her doctors, after taking a biopsy and making X-ray examinations, agreed that she was free from cancer. This, she said, had occurred five years ago, and she is now strong, vital and whole.

St. Kevin's Well

There was a crowd of tourists around a well. The guide pointed out five finger indentations, supposedly those of St. Kevin, in the rock. Visitors were asked to place a hand (left) in the rock, fitting the fingers exactly into the fissures of the rock, and then place it in the well beside it and make a specific prayer or request. The traditional belief is that the wish will be granted through the mediation of St. Kevin.

How his arthritic
hand was healed

There was an elderly man near the rock, and he told us that three years ago his hands had become crippled with arthritis, so much so that they were deformed. He followed the instructions by placing his hand on the rock and then in the well, begging St. Kevin to heal him. He said, "I was healed. Look at my hands now." They were perfect.

HOW DO ALL THESE HEALINGS TAKE PLACE?

Emerson says, "There is one mind common to all individual men. Every man is an inlet to the same and to all of the same. He that is once admitted to the right of reason is made a free man of the whole estate. What Plato has thought, he may think; what a saint has felt, he may feel; what at any time has befallen any man, he can understand. Who hath access to this universal mind is a party to all that is or can be done, for this is the only and sovereign agent."

For example, if an electrician is seeking answers to electrical or electronic problems, all the ingenuity, skill, research, discoveries and wisdom of Edison, Faraday, Marconi and others are in the repository of the universal mind, and everyone can tune in on their knowledge and wisdom. Any music ever played by Bach, Beethoven or Brahms is stored and deposited in the universal subjective mind, which animates all of us. Any musician can tune in and tap this reservoir, which is instantly available to all. The saints mentioned in religious literature are men and women who rose above their problems and appropriated more of Divinity than others. They rose to a higher point of spiritual awareness, and their healing consciousness and victories over all kinds of mental and physical diseases are deposited in the universal bank called the universal subconscious mind.

Therefore, when the Irishman prayed to St. Kevin, his imagination was fired, his consciousness was lifted up in faith and expectancy, and he tuned in on the healing vibrations always present in the universal mind. His prayer worked for him because his mind was full of faith and expectancy. His deep devotion, which was all-inclusive, impressed his subconscious mind and a healing followed.

Whatever you focus your attention on long enough to cause it to become impressed in your subconscious will in turn be demonstrated in your experience. This is the explanation for the so-called miracles which take place at St. Kevin's rock and well.

The Bible says, *And all things, whatever ye shall ask in prayer believing, ye shall receive* (Matt. 21:22). *Jesus said unto him, If thou canst believe, all things are possible to him that believeth* (Mark 9:23).

POINTS TO RECALL IN THIS CHAPTER

1. God's Healing Love can literally dissolve everything unlike itself in your mind and body. Love is the universal solvent. The gift of God within you is the Infinite Healing Presence, which is the only healing power there is.

2. You travel with God by claiming that the messengers of peace, love, light and beauty go before you making straight, glorious, joyous and happy your way. Know that God's love surrounds you in the heavens above and on the earth beneath, making all roads a safe highway.

3. The appearance of the Blessed Virgin at the Shrine of Fatima and other places is simply a dramatization of the subconscious mind of the children who claimed they saw the Virgin in a white robe in a tree. The Virgin in question resembles the picture in their prayer book or possibly the statue they saw in their church. It is a universal symbol for the female aspect of God or Divine Love.

4. People all over the world are healed at the various shrines, such as Shinto shrines, Buddha shrines, at Lourdes and at Fatima, as well as many other places. It is not the shrine or the waters or the relics that perform the so-called miracle, but firm faith, belief, great expectancy and a fired imagination, all of which, when prolonged over a period of time, impregnate the subconscious mind, releasing the Infinite healing power of the subconscious, which is the only healing power there is.

5. A miracle is not a violation of natural law. A miracle does not prove that which is impossible; it proves that which is possible. It is the response of your subconscious mind to your belief.

6. Spiritual healing is different from faith healing. For example, anything that moves the mind from fear to faith, such as a belief in the bones of saints, relics, holy waters, etc., may bring about a healing. Spiritual healing is the harmonious interaction of your conscious and subcon-

scious mind, scientifically directed. It is not the thing believed in, such as a shrine, relic, etc., but it is belief itself
which actually does the healing.

7. The apparitions of the "Lady" purported to have been
   seen at Fatima, Lourdes, Ireland and other places are subjective experiences induced by excitation, expectancy and
   auto-suggestion, which cause the subconscious mind to
   project an image in conformity with the pattern registered
   in the subconscious mind of the believer.

8. The future is already in our minds and may be seen by a
   clairvoyant or good psychic; so also is the future destiny
   of a nation. But as man learns to pray he can negate any
   negative happening that may be in his mind now. The
   future is your present thinking made manifest. Change
   your thought and you change your destiny.

9. When your vision is failing, ask yourself why your subconscious is selecting your eye as a scapegoat. What is it
   you wish to shut out of your world? Correct it at once,
   and a healing will follow.

10. When you pray for guidance and right action, and feel
    and know that God's Love surrounds you at all times and
    that God walks and talks in you, often a warning may
    come to you in a dream; and it is wise to obey the inner
    vision. You are seeing the event before it happens, and
    you can avoid it.

11. One way to impregnate your subconscious to secure
    wealth is to lull yourself to sleep every night with the
    words, "wealth is mine now." Wonders will happen in
    your life, and you will discover that your faith in your
    subconscious is your fortune.

12. The subconscious knows only the answer. If you don't
    have a penny in your pocket and you want to take a
    journey, turn your request over to your subconscious
    mind this way: "I am taking a trip to _____ in Divine
    order and everything I need is being provided now." Be-
    lieve and accept what you say as true, and it shall come
    to pass.

13. A man in London won money on the English Derby three
    years successively by lulling himself to sleep nightly for
    three months prior to the race by concentrating on one

word, "winner." His subconscious is all-wise, and it responded to his belief in its powers.

14. An ulcerated arm failed to heal until the victim decided to forgive himself and go free. The moment he ceased all self-condemnation a healing followed.

15. There is one universal mind. All the music ever played by great musicians is deposited in the universal mind and may be tapped by anyone. All the holy men of the world who triumphed over problems, difficulties and diseases of all kinds have also deposited their experiences and state of consciousness in the universal mind. All the wisdom and knowledge of Einstein, Faraday, Edison and Marconi are deposited in the universal bank of our mind and may be tapped by anybody interested in seeking answers. All he has to do is tune in. When you rise high enough in consciousness, the answer to your prayer will come. *And I, if I be lifted up from the earth, will draw all men* (manifestation) *unto me* (John 12:32).